My Journey & The Machine

My Journey & The Machine

How Internet Marketing Saved My Life...

Daniel Wagner

Cover Photo: Ric Bacon

MILESTONES

I.	Change Is Inevitable, Growth Is Optional...	7
II.	Why I Wrote This Book	17
III.	How I Wrote This Book	21

	The Journey	***25***
4.	One Of These Days	27
5.	The Promise	33
6.	Rock 'n' Roll, Drugs & Sex	39
7.	Peaks And Troughs	47
8.	Finding My Tribe	51
9.	Living On An Island	57
10.	Smoke And Mirrors (and The Holy Grail)	61
11.	A New Paradigm	65
12.	Almost Brave Enough	73
13.	What Do Millionaires Want?	77
14.	The Skin I'm In	83
15.	Other Mountains	89
16.	Onwards And Upwards	93
17.	I Don't Like Dogs	101

18.	Free-falling...	109
19.	...and Soft-landing	115
20.	Confused Sometimes Am I	121
21.	The Fast And The Furious	127
22.	One Of These Days	133
23.	Dropping The Parachute	139
24.	How I Started To Be-Lieve Again	143
25.	Getting Serious	147
26.	Becoming What You Are	153
27.	Deserve And Need	159
28.	Where In The World?	165
29.	The $250,000 Month	171
30.	The £100,000 Weekend	175
31.	Expanding Horizons	179
32.	Words And Deeds	183
33.	The End	187

Resources *191*

Introduction

Change Is Inevitable, Growth Is Optional...

'The greatest revolution in our generation is that of human beings, who by changing the inner attitudes of their minds, can change the outer aspects of their lives.' William James

Although you see my name on the cover of this book, this book is the work of hundreds of thousands of people, all coming out through my voice; through my words. And if there is wisdom and inspiration in this book, it is the inspiration of all of them together. So here are the 'Thank yous and acknowledgments'.

When I read a book, I love reading the 'Thank yous' because these are the people who influence the writer, the author. And I start, in no particular order, with some of the most widely-known heroes that inspired me, that I want to express my gratitude to. Some of these people don't know me from Adam but they are people that I want to thank first.

In my life as a public speaker, presenter, mentor, coach and trainer my goal is to inspire people to change their lives for the better just like my mentors and coaches did for me. I also know that many times the people you inspire and touch the most you never meet. They might pick up one of your talks or videos, they might be sitting at the back of the room or they might come across you through somebody telling your story.

With every one of the following people there is a story of coincidence and serendipity that lead me to them, and while it all appeared accidental at the time, looking back you see the trail.

First up there is Jim Rohn – in my eyes one of the greatest inspirational speakers who ever lived – who passed away 5th December 2009. His philosophies of success and life have changed my life and the life of many of my friends forever. I first studied his philosophy more than twenty years ago, but it took time for the seed to sprout and the roots to take hold and change my habits. If you want to check out Jim's work, I recommend his books 'The Five Major Pieces to the Life Puzzle' and 'Seven Strategies for Wealth & Happiness'. My favourite DVD set is 'How to Have Your Best Year Ever', which I must have watched a hundred times, discovering more truth and wisdom each time I imbibe it.

Then there is, of course, the great Tony Robbins, who, in May 2005, made me walk over glowing coals. I didn't know I had it in me. Little did I know it was the beginning of the end of a big chapter in my life; thank you, Tony. I personally think that Tony's books are not that great, but maybe check out 'Awaken the Giant Within'. However he really comes to life in his events or on his audio and video courses. His 'Personal Power' CD set was on auto replay for about five months of my life back in 2005. Tony influenced me so much and I 'modelled' him so closely, that I was called the 'Austrian Tony Robbins' for about a year when I first started public speaking.

There is T. Harv Eker, with his 'Secrets Of The Millionaire Mind'. This book really did change my life (again) and his 'Secret

Introduction

of the Millionaire Mind' cards I still use to this day almost everyday, enforcing the beliefs of the enlightened wealthy. I doubt Harv will ever read this book, so I can tell you that I didn't like him when I saw him on stage. (Sorry Harv). He came across aggressive and a bit full of himself when I saw him. But I have to say that the courses he puts together are pretty incredible! So I would not have flown to the US just to see Harv, but it was another of the coincidences that I was there with my employer, Hewlett Packard in the same week in the same town in April 2007. His discovery of the 'financial thermostat' is pure genius and to found out what held me back and stopped me from earning the money I deserved was deeply moving and disturbing! The process really works and I doubled and doubled and doubled again what I earned since 2007.

There is, of course, Roger Hamilton, the man who devised 'Wealth Dynamics'; a deep, philosophical and profound profiling system that finally relieved me from the pressure to be a 'balanced' person – one of the worst ideas our schooling system has ever forced onto poor, unsuspecting children like myself. His audio book 'Wink and Grow Rich' was on my iPod for months! But there are more lessons I learned from meeting Roger.

I remember clearly, in May, 2007, having been invited to a breakfast meeting with Roger Hamilton. Looking back, I can see how well constructed and orchestrated his sales presentation was, and how amazingly well these principles worked to influence people's (my) behaviour. I only understood the genius of Roger's presentation when I read one of the books that influenced my marketing and my business success the most, Robert Cialdini's 'Influence: The Psychology of Persuasion'.

The long and the short of it is, that I signed up for Roger Hamilton's XL life membership at $12,000; something I surely couldn't afford at that moment in time, but was keen to buy. I had just come back from T Harv Eker' 'Millionaire Mind' event in the US and I just saw it as a sign. What I learned from this experience is, that price is never a reason for people not to buy a product or service. It is always in your ability to demonstrate the benefits and creating desire for a product or service no matter what the price point is.

One of the best things that came out of me joining Roger's XL life partnership was the discovery of 'Wealth Dynamics', a wealth profiling system that allowed me to finally learn about my easiest path to wealth. After doing the test, I was presented with a view of myself of being a 'Star' and 'Creator'. Which explained why, over so many years, certain work appeared to be easy, or 'being in the flame', as Roger describes it, while many other tasks seemed to be tedious and hard work, what Roger describes to be 'in your wax'. I would encourage all of my readers to take the Wealth Dynamics test and learn more about their own easiest path to wealth. Looking back, I believe it was one of the major turnarounds in my journey from poverty and failure to success.

Some praise must go to Robert Kiyosaki's 'Rich Dad, Poor Dad' series. Another eye-opener to the mess our school system and traditional education path puts us in. 'The One Minute Millionaire' by Robert Allen and Mark Victor Hansen was another one of these incredible books. They literally fused and combined hundreds of books and knowledge of money and wealth creation into a compelling story and practical advice.

A massive, big, thank you also goes to Tim Ferriss. Not that I know Tim personally, but his book, 'The 4-Hour Work Week', has been one of those game-changers for me. Not just based on the philosophies that he shares in his book, but a lot through the

Introduction

practical and hands-on advice and resources that I could really start using – immediately – to get results. In 2007, when this book entered my life, it was one of the cornerstones, instrumental for the decision to change my life once more.

These are the celebrity heroes I can think of without trying... I am sure there are many more, and I don't want to walk over to my bookshelf which boasts literally hundreds of books with the words 'money, millionaire, rich, wealth' and similar in the title. If someone was willing to share to get wealthy, I wanted to know. And I am hoping that my contribution, this book, will find its way onto people's bookshelves and help shape their desires, and form part of their knowledge to journey towards the life of their dreams.

As I dedicated almost twenty years of my life to a spiritual group, I want to offer my respect and gratitude to my guru, who saved my life first, and who passed away while I was completing the book on 23rd February 2011. And to all my brothers and sisters at the time, with whom I experienced some of the most beautiful moments of my life in India and throughout the world. You know who you are.

I want to thank some of the unknown heroes that most of you will not know. And that includes my mum, who loved me no matter how much I messed up. Through my dark days and through my light days, it never mattered to her what I did; it only mattered who I was. There are people like Brent Curless, who was the first man to give me a job when I moved to the UK in 1995. He became a good friend, a business partner, and, to this day, one of my greatest inspirations. Only recently his book 'Younger Next Year' has been another breakthrough for me. To design my life the way I want it to be I sometimes need a kick up my back side!

A surprising 'thank you' is to my ex-wife, Clare, who will most likely not read this book but who I shared eighteen years of my life with. And, dare I say it, not the best bits. She put up with me in the most confused times of my life, the most unstable and most unbalanced, and she had witnessed my disappointment with myself and my frustration for many years. Without her, I wouldn't be where I am today. I know that things didn't work out the way we had planned, but to use a phrase much used in NLP, we 'did the best we could with the resources we had available to us'.

I want to thank some of the people who believed in me at a time when I didn't see who I was and what my potential was, and who saw something in me that I didn't yet see myself.

Mark Anastasi, who has been an inspiration and mentor, whose accidental recording of my case study in September 2006 became a cornerstone of my success;

Marcus de Maria, who was the first man to give me a speaking opportunity in 2007 and who has been a friend and mentor ever since;

Tamar Peters, who saw me on the stage at 'Wealth Intelligence Academy' with James Caan and booked me for a massive speaking gig for more than a thousand people in September 2008;

Dan Bradbury, whose confidence and certainty made me stretch myself and who was instrumental in me achieving what I have today;

Rob Moore, who came to my course in 2007 and has since been a friend and business partner;

Mike Southon, the Beermat entrepreneur, who's been encouraging me ever since I first met him and who was a guest speaker at my '7 Figure Formula' event in September 2010. He has shown me that business and life lessons can be so closely connected when I he presented his story of 'Something About The Beatles'.

I want to thank the hundreds who invested into me and my courses with their time and money; the many people I was able to help to change their lives and create a new lifestyle for themselves. And I also want to thank the thousands that have been in the audience laughing at my – sometimes terrible jokes – encouraging me, crying with me, laughing with me, and learning and making breakthroughs. I feel very privileged that you have been my audience, and want to thank you for the feedback that many of you have given me that I have a gift I needed to share.

And last but not least – and I know it is a corny phrase to end a chapter with – I want to thank my friends. It is those people who know me inside and out and where I never need to try. Steve Jones, who has been a close and trusted friend over twenty four years. Has has seen it all - the doubts and hopes, the trials and tribulations, the laughter and the tears. Thanks for your support and honesty, man! I feel privileged to have you in my life.

To Shan Verma, Shamir Rele, Urmil Patel and to Ric Bacon, who made me look so damn good on the cover photo. You are a master Ric, and I'll never forget the day of our photo shoot in October 2008.

It is people like James Watson, my business partner and friend; who over the last 2 years has been my sounding board and foil in most my business ventures. I don't take his loyalty and dedication for granted. And of course there is Licia, James' wife, who has taken care of me many times when I stayed in their house during the early days of 'buddies'. Phill Turner, who helped me get this book started. His admiration and believe in me made me believe it myself: I can do this! My friend of forty years, Tommy, who is always just asking how I am and never what I do or have, and Gregor in Austria, the first man I ever knew to become a millionaire from nothing, and the first man I ever knew to get paid more than $10,000 a day. You taught me loads. To Stuart Ross, who I met in 2010, one of the latest additions to my circle of friends and business partners.

And I want to, of course, thank Lieve, the wonderful gentle loving soul that came into my life more than two years ago. Everything changed to the better.

This section wouldn't be complete without 'the three Indians': Ranjan, Parmdeep, and Vanish. Most people confuse those names, and we have many funny stories of confusion, but my twenty years of meditation and familiarity with hindu and sanskrit names, I can at least tell them apart. Vanish for his many late nights back in 2004 with me on Skype explaining what marketing really was; Parmdeep for my first ever online project that actually made money in 2005; and Ranjan for his invaluable business lessons and guidance that finally made me understand that there was no conspiracy against me to make money; I just didn't know what I was doing.

This book is based on my life, experiences and recollections. In some cases names of people, places, dates and details of events have been changed to protect the privacy of others.

I hope that this book can help you achieve the life of your dreams, and possibly nudge you – just that little bit – over the edge to make the decision you were about to make, to not give up on your dreams just yet, and not to give up on yourself – ever. It is a road worth traveling. It's a goal worth pursuing. And as for your life and what you can make of it? It's your call and as far as I know, we've only got one shot at it.

And lastly to my kids Siddhartha and Alice, two amazing beings who had to accept what I decided was best for them. I wanted to be the best dad for you there ever was, and be the dad I never had. I have made mistakes, I have failed in many ways, but I always have and always will love you for who you are. You don't have to be anything or anyone for me, you're both perfect just the way you are. May your journey to meaning and happiness be quicker than mine.

Daniel Wagner, February 2011

Pre-preface

Why I Wrote This Book

'I find television very educating. Every time somebody turns on the set, I go into the other room and read a book.' Groucho Marx

What I love about books is that the reader chooses to consume them at their pace. In their way. Being able to re-read, read slowly, skip, jump around, or even start at the end gives power to you, the reader. How superior to film and television, where you are forced the pace and speed of the creator!

Much of my learning has come from books, even in the 21st century. So why did I write this book? Now, there are a couple of reasons. When I embarked to write this – 'my' – book, I did it with the desire to become part of people's lives, their library, their conversations and thoughts. A micro legacy I suppose.

I always wanted to be an author, and the reality is that for four years I've been telling myself that I'm going to get it done, just didn't get round to it and didn't have a clue how to do it. So some things on your to-do list just travel with you – for years – until it just gets ridiculous and one day (and that day is today) I said to myself: 'that's it - I'll do it now!'

If you're worried about how to do it, just check out my other chapter, 'How I wrote this book', and you might realise that it's not as hard as you think. Saying that though, at the time of writing these words the book is far from being 'done' - so this is wishful thinking at its best. But the fact that there are hundreds of thousands of books out there tells me it can't be that hard. So I'm just gonna have to find a way to get it done!

Another reason why writing a book is a good thing for almost everyone – and I will explain more later when we talk about marketing, and the market you're working in – is what we call 'lead generation'. A book is a great calling card. A book is a great way to get people to learn more about you, which will build connection and hopefully trust: the basis for transactions; the basis for life-long relationships; the basis for real customer value.

A book also gives you instant authority when you enter a room or conversation. It gives you authority when you go for a meeting and you slap it on the table and just let it rest there, to make its own impression.

I also think that every human being has a unique story worth telling, and this book is my story. I know it will inspire and help people, as other books have inspired and helped me. I am now one of the many people with the aspiration to help and change people's lives through words, beware, here it comes.

One more important reason why I write this book is for myself. A very simple and selfish reason because I want to read my own story as an observer and witness, and out of that, I will be learning about myself and who I am.

Writing this book was indeed a 'journey' in itself and many of the events I had to dig up and poke around in triggered more than uncomfortable feelings. But there were also moments of intense beauty and insights that were almost forgotten as I delved into their recollection, I am glad I found them again. It also addresses a recurring theme and topic of 'being enough' and deservedness, that

I battle with all my life. 'how dare I write a book, what have I got to share?' These moments of self doubt were scattered throughout the whole project, and every day I sat down to write or edit, the same conversation entered my mind.

Harv Eker taught me a great way to deal with this disempowering self talk: Just say 'Thanks for sharing'. I guess one of the reasons why this project wasn't abandoned (and I thought about it many times) was because of my public commitment to it and the friends that have dedicated their time to help me. Phill, Keith and James, thank you for your support and time.

I have plans to get into the Amazon bestseller list with this book. You might chuckle and think I am arrogant, deluded, or just plain crazy, but I want to do it more as proof for the power of marketing. I understand there are hundreds of 'better books' being written all the time, I understand that I have no publisher and no book shops backing me, but I also know that I know a thing or two about marketing, and I have done successful product launches. So when you read this book, you might be one of the great people that helped me become a best selling author on Amazon. Thanks guys! I hope you'll enjoy the read.

Preface

How I Wrote This Book

'All Tasks Expand Naturally To Their Given Deadline.'
Daniel Wagner

How, indeed, do you write a book? First I googled 'how to write a book' and marvelled at the options. Then I devoured two books about how to write a book, and then I spoke to some of the enlightened human beings who have actually done it.

One guy locked himself in a room for three months (not too attractive). Another one suggested a bit of self discipline, getting up thirty minutes earlier every day to write a page a day, and within four months you'll have 120 pages (I could never do that).

The ghost writer concept really appealed to me, but the first two attempts were terrible. I couldn't put my name to it – no way. And who knows me like I know myself?

Then I had this great idea to have some of my many talks and interviews transcribed, thinking that with lots of source material it would be easy to distill the nuggets. That wasn't working either, as there was a lot of repetition and no flow. I thought of a kind of book being just transcripts of some random ramblings. Scrap that.

One of my last attempts was working with a 'book midwife', who told me after two encouraging meetings that she wanted me to part with £5,000 and wanted to co-own my book. That didn't happen.

Actual what inspired me were two of my Mastermind students, Robin Shaw and Alan Robinson who are writing a book as part of my coaching! So I wanted to write a book as well. But looking at the process they were going through I wanted a shortcut. So my obsessive and addictive nature got the better of me! I decided to do it in a less than three weeks. Sounds like a crazy idea and all you need to make a crazy idea happen is to find a crazy person who would commit to it with you. And I found that person in Phill Turner.

When we set out to achieve what, in my mind, was an impossible task, I knew that there were three things that would make me succeed, and I use those three things every time I want to make progress. First I set a hard deadline, second, I choose an accountability buddy, and third I make a public commitment. In my case to my Inner Circle Mastermind Group.

So when I spoke to Phill Turner he immediately agreed (that's the kind of guy he is). Phill is a man who helps you get things done. To use the slogan of an 'Adidas' advertising campaign 'impossible is nothing!'. So writing a book – an impossible task with no plan – came together in less than three weeks. And that's how I wrote my book. We had less than four weeks from start to finish as I want to have it ready for my time on stage at the Property Super Conference on 6th March, my 'hard deadline'.

I have so many times gone over the content I wanted to write in my head that we did the following. I did a little outline, closed my eyes and in my mind's eye imagined reading the book that was to be written. I found it pretty easy to speak as if I were reading, and

Preface

what you have in front of you is some of that first draft, recorded over nine hours on the 5th and 6th February 2011.

My book 'writing' setup. 5th February 2011, 8:15 am. Whiteboard, flip chart, laptop and microphone, notepad and a glass of water. And not a clue what to do next. The book went to print on 24th February 2011.

I'm not saying you can or should write your book that way, because maybe your mind doesn't work that way, or you don't know a guy like Phill or you don't have the deadline or reason to do it, but all I am saying is that when the time is right, things 'just happen'; or as Jim Rohn would correct me: 'Things don't just happen, things happen - just'.

There are many ways to skin a cat, as they say. And there are many ways to write a book. You don't need a typewriter anymore, that's for sure and you don't need to worry about publishing houses and printers. Yo can simply go to Amazon's 'Create Space' or lulu.com. I have not opened a blank Word document, because, to be honest, opening a blank white page doesn't inspire me – it intimidates me. So I got started with a recording and some transcripts, and once I got going, there was no stopping me until I had arrived.

So get started, find an accountability buddy, create a deadline, tell everyone about it and you'll get it done.

Everything, they say, is created twice. First in your mind, then in the world.

I bet you created your book once already and I bet you've mentioned it a few times to your mates – now it's time to get it out there a second time. The world is waiting and you will be rewarded for what it will make of you to write your book.

The Journey

Chapter 1

One Of These Days

'You can't always get what you want. But if you try sometimes you might find – You get what you need.' The Rolling Stones

It's the 25th of December, 2008, and it's four o'clock in the afternoon. I'm taking a photo of myself and, looking at the photo, I look terrible. And you know what? I feel it as well. How did I end up here? My life was supposed to be perfect; I was a speaker on stage, I was highly paid, and people were seeing at me as a role model. My story was supposed to inspire everyone else to follow in my footsteps. From where I stand today, I wouldn't wish anyone to feel like I do today. Alone, rejected, misunderstood, without direction or purpose. I worked hard and made sacrifices to get here, was it all in vain? I had promised myself to not spend another Christmas alone, but like other promises I had made to myself before, this one was broken, too. So how did I end up at this place of utter despair?

Let me just rewind a few months. All summer I was trying to go out with Monica, a girl I had fancied for many years. And we had one magical day and I forever wanted to recreate this one day – without success. Monica had been my hairdresser for many years, and had been my fantasy for so long that it wasn't even real. So I pursued her for months; I did whatever I could. I courted her, and I was the nicest guy. Brought her coffee in the mornings, picked her up for lunch, spent every evening with her and many times the

27

night. As a friendship goes, it was great, but I was fixated with making it something else.

You see, after twenty years in my religious group to go out or even get to know a girl who drank, swore, smoked and was sexy was such an incredibly exciting thing – I was mesmerised and hypnotised. Like a moth to a flame. I didn't let go, it was an effort, I admit that, but finally, towards the end of the October, she agreed to go out with me. And why is this relevant? Because I pushed so hard. And in a way, deep inside, I knew she wasn't the one, but I was attracted by how she looked and how she behaved and how she stood out from the rest. And in a way it was the chase. I understand, looking back, that all I wanted was to win; all I wanted was to have that success, that boost for my battered ego and self confidence. It wasn't about a 'relationship' at all. I didn't actually have a clue how to have a relationship.

So autumn was a great time. I felt I was getting closer to the prize. I felt I was getting closer to my goal. And as I pushed, and as I forced myself and forced her into situations and the life that I thought I wanted to lead with her, I came to the realisation that, deep inside, my soul was torn. I felt extremely insecure around her and permanently waited for bad news to happen.

I cried; I hadn't cried for years. I cried because I was lonely. I cried because I was disillusioned. I cried because I felt that I had betrayed myself. I don't believe in soul, as such, but I felt that I had 'sold my soul'. I had given up who I was to achieve something that I thought people wanted me to achieve. I felt I acted on outside pressure. Whose pressure was this?

So how did I end up, on Christmas day, totally in pieces? Leading up to Christmas, I had just rented an expensive penthouse

Chapter 1

flat for me and my son, but with the prospect of having Monica move in with me. It gave me a bit of a stomach ache to spend so much money on living accommodation because I'd always been very careful with money, especially when it had to do with anything for myself. I'm a generous guy I think, but spending on myself was always difficult.

So I moved into this amazing place. It was big with many empty rooms. I had no furniture, so I went out and I bought what I thought she would love. And I thought, "If I make this place right, she'll move in with me". Everything was set: the big leather furniture, I bought a big plasma TV. I never had one before, but I thought, "That looks good". I bought a new car. You know, I had some money, so I thought, "Hey, let's use it. Let's impress someone".

And it worked, to a degree. I felt in my gut that something was wrong, but I just ignored that little voice. I had chosen to let myself be guided by greed and lust more than by my sixth sense guiding me towards my well-being. Many times I was suspicious that something was going on, but finally, on that day, on the day before Christmas, on Christmas Eve, things really blew up.

I haven't mentioned that it was my second Christmas without my family after the divorce, and I had spent my first Christmas alone in London in a Lebanese Restaurant eating carrot soup. Not my favourite memory.

On Christmas Eve in the afternoon, she was expected to come round and we were meant to spend the most beautiful, romantic Christmas together. (Monica as a Czech and me being Austrian means we celebrate Christmas Eve). She didn't turn up at the agreed time. So, after hours of deliberating and being worried, I finally drove down to her flat, and as I arrived I had the shock of my life. Looking up, I saw her in the arms of another guy; she in tears, he talking at her. I didn't know what to do. She hadn't noticed me yet, so I was just hiding; watching. I didn't know what had happened, but I did know something had just gone terribly wrong. I felt like a coward, sneaking back to my car and driving away. My heart was aching and my mind was racing.

I went back to the flat and waited for her for an hour, or maybe two. I had the craziest thoughts and my imagination played total havoc with me. Then I drove to her house again, at this point, knocking at her door, trying to confront her. I was shaken, I was in tears, I was angry. I had realised that I had just lost something that I thought I owned. I lost something I thought was really important to me. Mainly, what I had lost, though, was a distraction from myself. And mainly I was afraid to be alone – again.

As you might guess, she wasn't spending Christmas with me after all. So that evening when I was alone in this big flat, with everything laid out for Christmas, the food bought and uncooked, the alcohol in the fridge. I didn't drink. I hadn't consumed alcohol for twenty years before that night. Well – that changed – I drank a whole bottle of vodka, enriched with a four pack of Red Bull. I couldn't sleep that night. I wrote my Christmas story, five thousand words of coming to terms with my situation. Digging deep to understand why and how this happened. Needless to say I spent half the night on the toilet, just wanting to die. I didn't quite know what had hit me. Wasn't I supposed to be successful? Wasn't I supposed to be happy? Didn't I have the life I always wanted? Not quite. Shouldn't I know better? Apparently not.

Around lunch time the next day – I drove down to her house again. I wanted to really clear the situation up. I felt in pain – not just from what I'd done to myself the night before, but the emotional pain of disappointment and disillusionment; the emotional pain of loneliness; and the emotional pain of knowing that I had to start from scratch. I had no foundation, no basis, and I had no meaning.

This is the infamous Christmas Day photo I took just outside her house on the 25th. I have used it in my stage presentations for the last two years.

Besides – the money in the bank had no meaning either (It was the first time in my life I had a six figure bank account!). The large flat had no meaning. The 50" plasma TV definitely had no meaning. What really was missing was a real relationship with someone that I could build on, someone I could trust. Like a child, that morning, I wept once more. And like a child, that morning, I threw away everything that was reminding me of our relationship. I destroyed the pictures that we made together. I threw away everything that had anything to do with her, but it didn't help how I felt, it didn't take away the pain.

At that moment in time, when I felt the loneliest since I was a young boy, I made a decision. Let me re-phrase that. I didn't make a decision. A decision was made for me. Something inside of me, as clear as a bell, spoke to me. I don't want you to freak out on me; I don't mean voices coming out of me and talking to me, but what I mean is that I had clarity. And this clarity can only happen in deep moments of inspiration or desperation. For me, it was the latter one.

I knew I would not compromise myself in the future in relationships. I knew I wouldn't compromise my 'soul' again. I would not compromise my ideals, what I stand for and what I stand against, and that gave me incredible strength and determination. It was Christmas Day, and I was alone. It was Christmas Day in 2008 when my life changed once more. Although I was perceived to be successful, from the outside, I knew that what really mattered was to be successful on the inside. That day was a turnaround for me to start living as who I really was. I finally understood that the true meaning of life is honesty to yourself and the people around you, the meaningful relationships you can create, and I was on my way to get myself just that.

But let's go back to a small town in Austria some forty years ago, to see how it all began...

Chapter 2

The Promise

'One reason so few of us achieve what we truly want is that we never direct our focus; we never concentrate our power. Most people dabble their way through life, never deciding to master anything in particular.'
Tony Robbins

Growing up in Austria or in broader terms in the western world sets you up for disappointment; The reality is that we all grow up with a big promise that is not to be fulfilled for most. What we see in the papers, what we see on TV, what we hear, and the stories that are being told around us, set us up with a big promise; set us up with ideals and dreams of how our life should be – from perfect relationships, to abundance in financial resources, to abundant health and a long life. And that is how we set out on our path, expecting things to 'just work out'. This is why we end up being obsessed with eternal youth, financial freedom, accumulating material goods and much more. We live in the belief of entitlement – a misguided misconception. So, like most of us, I wanted it all because I deserved it, as a matter of birth right. I had no clue how to get my hands on any of it, prosperity, happiness or well-being, and neither school nor my parents had any answers.

I grew up in an average, simple, bourgeois environment, with my parents being good to me and good to each other. Money was never an issue. Don't get me wrong, that didn't mean it wasn't a big issue – it was just simply never discussed. Looking back and knowing what I know now, that was one of the reasons why having any money eluded me for so long; I didn't learn how to master the laws of money is and how money worked. My father was kind of invisible, always working and never home, a pattern that I unconsciously adopted in my own life and marriage later on.

From what I heard and remember I was a happy child, always trying to help people and making them laugh. I am not sure when this pattern was set, maybe even when I was a baby. My theory is that we have a way of getting our parents' or mother's attention or love, and whatever works first, becomes unconsciously our primary way of getting love and attention even in our adult lives.

I have observed my own and many other people's behaviour to back this theory up, and maybe it even has a name, but all it means that we are pretty much using one strategy to get attention and connection. Mine is helping people. Tony Robbins talks about your primary question that you ask yourself all the time. What is yours?

Early on in my childhood I was encouraged to do whatever I wanted and I found everything easy. Life was easy. And many of you can surely relate to that, looking back on your childhood, that things were easy; you are in flow and everything is just there. Nobody seems to want anything from you; you're just living. I believed, that I was divine and that I was invincible; I would never die; I would never get ill. Maybe that's just me, but I think it is a child's normal state of mind.

My earliest memories are when I was four or five; I don't know what happened before, but I guess it was all good. (It seems crazy how much effort you put into those first years with your kids and they don't even remember any of it). My earliest memories are of a friendship with a guy called Tommy, still a friend of mine to this

Chapter 2

day. I grew up in a high rise tower block in the industrial part of Innsbruck called Reichenau (ironically meaning meadow of the rich and yet we were broke). I remember that Tommy and I had visions that we wanted to change the world in a big way. Forty years later I am a public speaker and marketer and Tommy is a neurologist. Have we changed the world? I guess in our own small way we have, but not the way we planned.

School was great. Six years old, my first day at school, and I loved it. I was so eager to learn. The potential and the promise of everything was just immense, and I was excited and knew it would be just a matter of time until I 'knew it all'. I was a great student and an easy student to have. I can easily memorise things; I learned and picked up things very fast, and I was the best in class for years. Between the age of six and ten life was a breeze. Everyone seemed to love me, I seemed to love life, and everything was awesome. At this tender age I hadn't spent a single thought on what I wanted to do later in life. I was sure that things would 'just work out' no matter what. An attitude I still have today, even after all the challenges and failures.

If I look around at what people say they want, most of them mention the same three things: freedom, love and choice.

Everyone wants 'freedom', normally not defined in any clear terms. I define it as freedom of choice; to do what I want, when I want to do it, and – if I'm really lucky – who I want to do it with. But I also found in my life that having freedom with no restraints, or freedom without structure, can easily make you feel at a loss because human beings, it seems, need some sort of structure.

What else do people want? We want love; we want somebody in our life that shows us that we're appreciated. And I had loads of that when I was young. I felt appreciated in all I was and whatever I did. But when I grew older, I struggled with feeling worthy of love or appreciation.

Thirdly, it seems that we love choice. My simple assumption is – and I read many books and psychological studies about it – that too much choice paralyses people. Too much choice – and we certainly live in an age of too much choice in the 21st century – limits your ability to find true happiness. Or in simple terms – unlimited choice creates unhappiness. If you can have whatever you want – then nothing has special meaning anymore. We can see this pattern with celebrities and stars, who live miserable lives of ultimate choice with no meaning.

So the first chapter of my life – the early memories of friendship and being appreciated, the easy years of school – they are my foundation. And I know that with all the confusion that was to follow, this foundation gave me something to fall back on, something to build on. I felt that I would make a big impact on the world around me, and I was told I had a gift. I was told that I had charisma that could touch people's lives. I knew that when I was in a group I could, with my energy, change how the group felt. And it was beautiful. It made me feel alive! I was a good guy and I liked it.

I clearly remember a day though when I was about twelve years old – I was in secondary school back then – when I started getting attracted to the wrong crowd. Now, don't ask me why and how it happened because I really, plainly, don't know. I seem to remember that I started to get fed up of being the good kid; the one that everyone loved; the one that found everything easy. It was almost like I tried to create difficulty for myself. I seemed to try to create adversity – to make my life more interesting, more challenging.

Chapter 2

I'm not exactly sure why, but I started at an early age to get into drugs. I remember that the people who took drugs interested me – there was something dark and mysterious about them. And the simplicity and lightness of early childhood was exchanged for an attraction to the dark and mysterious.

Looking back, I would say my 'seeking years' had started then. Somehow I knew that the illusion of happiness as a child would be replaced with the mundane existence of most people in the western world, working on the hamster wheel of a job, forever looking for the next pay rise, or a little break or escape from their daily chores.

I understood more about my parents' life; I understood that money was short; I understood that they couldn't do what they wanted.

I read between the lines, and listened between the words and I saw and heard the disappointment and fear and the smallness of their own lives; the goals they never achieved. I heard blame and I heard justifications. Somehow I knew there was something wrong with that philosophy. Was there a better way?

All I knew was that I didn't want what they had. And, in simple terms, I grabbed the next best thing; the one thing that looked different to everything else I saw. What had opened up for me is what I call 'the void'. What people wanted me to be and what I wanted, were starting to be two very different things; two completely different worlds. My self-image started to be split in two. I still had, of course, the sweetness and innocence of childhood in me, but I also was a young adult looking for adventure and danger because life was just too easy; it was just too good. I'm not sure you can relate to this. I don't know what your life story or your childhood was like, but for me, I knew that life would never be the same.

I started slipping at school. I started producing results that were not the best I could; and I started to use schemes and lies to not go to school at all. Today they are funny stories, back then they were clever little schemes of betrayal. I started to live in two worlds. One happy illusion I kept up for my mum and dad and school, and then – the other secret, sad reality of my real life. Somehow I relished in the secretiveness of this existence; somehow I enjoyed the excitement of knowing that nobody knew but me. But if you've ever been in that place, or know of somebody who lived like this, you also know that not being honest with yourself or the world creates loneliness, disillusionment, and separation from who you really are.

In my early years, happiness eluded and there can be no true happiness in deceit.

Chapter 3

Rock 'n' Roll, Drugs & Sex

'Pain and death are part of life. To reject them is to reject life itself.' Henry Ellis

You might wonder why this chapter is called 'Rock and Roll, Drugs, and Sex'. It seems to be the wrong way around, but that's the order that I was introduced to the world of adulthood.

I was 12 years old when I started playing music. I picked up the guitar; I was in love with The Beatles and their music. At that time, it made me strive – and it made me seek. It made me understand that there is so much more to life than I had experienced in my little town, in Innsbruck, living with my parents. I learned English at school and I used my dictionary to understand what John and Paul were saying and singing about; I could access eight years of their music at once; a condensed life story from their first song to the last. I think it fast-tracked my growing up. I rushed along from the innocent 'Love me do' to the final cut – 'The End', the last song on Abbey Road.

I didn't understand it back then, but I get it now. John (I'm pretty sure it's John who wrote it) summed up in pretty much one line what life is all about:

'And In The End, The Love You Take Is Equal To The Love You Make'.

When I was fourteen I spent four to five hours every day playing music and writing songs with my best friend, Werner. We started writing our own songs and, to this day I write songs to explore my inner world. The magic of writing songs or writing poetry or making music is that, unconsciously, unknowingly, you slip into this space of inspiration. Spontaneity and improvisation force you to draw from a deeper source; not your intellect; not your thoughts. You get into this moment, this movement called 'the flow'. This is how I later on recognised the value of meditation, which in its own way, helps you to get into the present moment.

Werner Hofmann and me recording our own songs for our first radio show in 1982. Notice the matching outfits and mullet

Music – that was what I wanted. It was a way for me to reach people, touch people, and connect with people. And we started playing to our friends. We started writing songs, and very soon, at the age of fifteen, for the first time, I played on national radio. We

Chapter 3

could present our songs; and we won a competition for our compositions. I already saw myself as a pop star. I already saw myself on the big stage with people waving their candles and waving their lighters to the ballads that moved their souls. I had a plan, and what I loved about it, was that it was different and it was special. I always wanted to be special.

I also noticed that playing music seemed to have an impact on the opposite sex. It was the first time that I properly paid attention to the girls out there. Music seemed to make it easy to get off with them.

I very quickly found my love for sex. I liked the idea of having intense emotional moments and sex seemed to fulfil that. Just like the music, I seemed to be able to enter this space of the present when I was with girls. Life was getting very exciting indeed. I wasn't very steady in my relationships, to say the least, because I always looked for the next girl, the next chase; the next hit; the next high. There was always somebody I thought was better or more exciting. And this is when, for the first time, I understood the little saying, 'the grass is always greener over there' – as every new promise also held its very own share of disappointment. It took me another thirty years before I added to that phrase, 'but you still have to mow it'. Because it doesn't matter – whatever you have, there is something called 'maintenance' or something called 'reality'.

Puberty had taken its toll, and my skin looked more like an outbreak of measles than my normal skin that you see today. I wasn't highly confident because it seemed like my body – some parts – had grown out of proportion; especially my nose. I didn't feel that great about it myself and with my voice breaking the singing career was on hold for a while as well. I also realised that the ease of living that I experienced earlier in my life had gone. I seemed to be torn; I don't know into how many pieces, but I didn't seem to be in flow, it didn't feel like I was one. I felt awkward.

That is the time when I was attracted to, and started taking, drugs; the third addition to 'sex, drugs, and rock and roll', or in my order, 'rock and roll, sex, and drugs'. It seemed to be the logical next step on my journey to looking for more meaning. Within a very short time, I consumed copious amounts of drugs every day. I started to deal because that seemed to be a logical way to become supplier and be supplied. Of course, as with every addiction, there was never an end in sight. I spent most of my days consuming, acquiring, or chasing the elusive high. I became the biggest dealer in my school, pushing weed, dope and LSD in the breaks.

At first, drugs seemed to have the effect I was looking for. Enhancing my perception of reality, gaining access to less obvious angles and exploring philosophies of existence previously hidden from my experience. But it soon wore off. I look at it today like a bank loan. You get experiences through drugs like you get money from a bank. But you got to check the small print. You will have to pay back with interest, and some serious hidden fees at times.

At the ages of sixteen and seventeen, I was, maybe, the unhappiest I've ever been so far. Knowing what I didn't want, but not a clue what I wanted; angry with the world; angry against an unknown and undefined enemy, which I called 'the establishment'. Now, that is very common, I believe, for young people today as it was back in the '80s. It is as common here in the UK as it is in Europe, but I seemed to be a particularly bad example of a disillusioned and dissatisfied young person. I started to be involved in the petty crimes associated with drugs as well – and justified it

Chapter 3

with ease. It is amazing how one can bend reality to fit one's needs! I sold myself onto the most ludicrous and outlandish ideas.

It was at that time, just before I turned seventeen, when I fell in love for the first time. Meaningless, short, mainly sexual relationships were replaced by a true connection with a deeper part of myself. The girl I met – Patrizia, was twenty four and from South Tyrol, a province now belonging to Italy but with Austrian heritage. She was an orphan who never knew her father, and had lost her mother to cancer when she was only six years old. Brought up by her jealous and loveless half sister she learned to stand on her own two feet very early on in life.

My favourite photo I took of Patrizia when we met in 1983. I had lost all photos a few years later but she had kept a copy which I obtained in 2009. This image was my vision of the perfect woman as long as I can remember.

Meeting her was a game changer. I remember being totally immersed in being together with her, but still inexperienced and foolish. My mum wasn't pleased when Patrizia moved in with me. I was still at school and seventeen, but I was quite strong willed and made a compelling case. Patrizia brought a lot to my life – tenderness, humility and spirituality; and of course her books on freedom. I remember distinctly reading Jiddu Krishnamurti's 'Freedom from the Known' and Hermann Hesse's 'Siddhartha'; it was like a veil had lifted. It was like a new magical opportunity opened up; a new promise. And from the age of seventeen I became a spiritual seeker – a drug addict, but with a deep sense of searching. It was the first time that I failed to attempt to give up drugs and its side effects that had taken hold of me.

Looking back, it seems sad that I couldn't make that relationship work. I never stopped loving Patrizia and maybe it's simply Cat Stevens' 'The First Cut Is The Deepest' wisdom, that shaped my experience and created a benchmark for all future relationships. There was so much promise and potential, but I was never able to fulfil it because of my addiction and inexperience. I have cried many tears for myself and my weakness of not being able to give up drugs for her and me back then. For the next twenty years though, every time I came to Innsbruck I was looking for her, sometimes imagining seeing her and often dreaming of her.

The next four years are a little bit of a blur. I believe it's mainly due to the fact that I was, most times, in a state of 'high'; or you could call it a 'low' at this stage as consuming drugs every day does not give you any experience of a heightened awareness.

I was damn lucky not to contract HIV or Hepatitis C from the Heroine needles and I am pretty lucky that my nose survived the Cocaine onslaught when I was nineteen. A few brief moments of clarity amongst many days of deep confusion on LSD, showed me that there was a possible experience of happiness, but I was obsessed with the idea of finding that happiness inside myself and

Chapter 3

not inflicted through chemical potions. Not a single day went by that I didn't think or talk about kicking my habit.

One particular person seemed to be a kind of guide for me at this stage, a 'guru', and, ironically, I only met him again by chance a few weeks ago after over twenty years. He introduced me to more spiritual literature. Not from the Indian tradition, like my girlfriend, but more from the South American tradition. The Carlos Castaneda books became my new 'religion' and I was convinced that I could escape the cycle of birth and re-birth through the teachings presented in the books. Most people believe these books are fiction, but me and my friends were convinced they were secret teachings we could follow.

Talking of religion, most Austrian kids are born into a religious life to a degree. I was Roman Catholic like 90+% of Austrians, but my family didn't go to church apart from at Christmas. My mum is Jewish and my dad is Protestant, but they thought baptising me as a Roman Catholic would be less conspicuous.

I always found church boring and fake and religious studies a real wind up for me, so when I was given the opportunity at fourteen I made a clear choice to stop religious studies. I was a young intellectual philosopher and opposed the church and any established religion. I just didn't want to have to believe in anything, I wanted proof and experiences. I thought it made no sense that being born in a country defined your religion and therefore defined your view of the world.

So, as mentioned, between the ages of seventeen and twenty one, life was a bit of a blur; trying to escape the claws of the drug addiction; seeking and searching for purpose and spirituality in books, and relationships, something that had eluded me up to now.

I had no clue what I wanted to do with my life, but I knew I had a yearning for meaning, purpose, and fulfilment.

Finding it though was still a long way off.

Chapter 4

Peaks And Troughs

'In the mountains, the shortest way is from peak to peak: but for that you must have long legs.' Friedrich Nietzsche

I kind of managed to scrape through school; I spent most of my time devising ways to cheat the system. That I somehow passed my exams it is a miracle. But I needed to get away from Innsbruck, and the best way I could think of was to tell my parents I wanted to study in a different city. I knew they wanted me to study, it was one of their broken records I heard ever since I was ten. 'We want you to have it better than us, you can study at university!' Little did they know that I didn't intend to graduate. I just wanted to get away and get some money to live while I tried to work out what was going on. I hoped that a new environment, away from my drug friends would make my life easier.

So there I was in Salzburg, 200 miles away from my home town, Innsbruck, 'studying' communication science and philosophy. To give you an idea just how confused I was about what I wanted or – thought I wanted – let me run you through the subjects I tried. Every term, I tried something else: I started with Latin; don't ask me why. I hated it at school, but I just thought it would be cool to study Latin. I hated it at uni too. Then I tried architecture. I liked the idea of building something, something like a legacy that has longevity. But it was boring as hell, and I didn't last even a term. Then I thought, Italian (It was the Italian girls that

I thought of more than any other practical application). So I studied Italian. Again, I didn't succeed; or should I say, I gave up. Then, how about, 'Science of Language'. I really enjoyed the name of that subject; I thought to get to the bottom of the meaning of words would help me to find the meaning of life itself – guess what? Again, it was so boring that I gave up.

So after two years of being at university, I had not gotten anywhere. My last attempt to find anything slightly useful and easy (that was my main criterion now), was to study 'Communication Science'. I was told it was easy pickings and I could convince my parents to keep paying for me with the prospect of me studying. When I say 'studying', I mean smoking weed all day, and once a week making it to uni. I remember in my third year when I found the library. It was amazing! This was where they were all hiding! I had no clue what I was doing, I had no ideas what I wanted to become or what any of it was about! I was attracted to girls like a monkey to a banana and I went from one short and intense relationship to another.

I definitely hadn't achieved 'happiness'. As I grew more desperate, I started to look around, and I started to consciously seek out spiritual groups. During a period of just three months at the end 1986, I explored everything I could find: Pentecostals, Adventists, Jehovah's Witnesses, Chinmoy, an Indian guru. They all left me distinctly unimpressed. I didn't believe they had the answer, I felt they were kidding themselves. The last one on the list was a group that taught the path of the 'parasympathetic yoga'. I remembered vaguely, from my school, that the parasympathetic nervous system was the part of our system that was automated, outside our control. I liked the idea that something would happen to me automatically and was not based on my thoughts, my deductions of logical thoughts or actions. I liked it because I seemed to only be capable of getting myself into a mess but not out of it.

The group I found followed an Indian guru, a lady who is believed to be an incarnation of the Holy Ghost. How weird is that? It was so unlike me to join a religious group!

I had stopped religious studies at fourteen. I left the Catholic church at eighteen. I signed myself out and was without religion, which I was really proud of. So there I was, three years later, joining a strong Hindu group with one simple aim: to reach enlightenment. I was attracted to the group for various reasons: it was free, and the people seemed nice and friendly and all looked happy. I really didn't have much to lose so I threw myself into it. What I loved about the meditation that I started in February 1987 is that it gave me a big enough goal to get my teeth into. I mean, 'enlightenment' – how much bigger can it get? The ultimate meaning of life. On the first evening, Tuesday 24th February 1987, according to the group, my 'Kundalini' was awakened and would start to guide me to an enlightened life if I was to allow it and help it through meditation. Sounded all good to me so far!

I felt some peaceful moments practising at home and decided to go back to the group, which met every week in Salzburg. In week three though I met Brigitte, a twenty six year old Mother of two, and I fell in love. The meditation suddenly was a lot less important and enlightenment could wait. Two weeks later, I moved in with her.

I lived through six months of oblivious happiness, before in August '87 I had a major realisation. I had decided to spend the summer in Spain on a small island with 'good supply' (read drugs) off Cadaques near Figueres. Some friends had told me about this hippie island and I wanted to see it for real. I lived in the true spirit of the sixties in a ruin of a castle with about fifty other people, mainly stoned out of our brains, sharing everything we had, from drugs to girls to the food we found on the island. It was on that Island that I had a disturbing and recurring dream about my life. I had lost my heart and mind and was a soulless shell. I woke up every day noticing how weak and powerless I had become. Every day I woke up telling my friends that I would stop taking drugs that day, and every day I ended up taking them. Every day I told my friend we would go and climb a nearby hill and everyday we failed to do it.

Then a weird thing happened. I started to remember the words and knowledge gleaned from my meditation. I started to remember the people and the lady. It was almost like this energy they had talked about had started to talk to me. One morning, after three weeks of failed attempts to climb the hill or stop taking drugs, I just packed my bags and hitch hiked all the way to Austria, to find the people from the meditation group.

I was ready to learn more.

Chapter 5

Finding My Tribe

'If you change the way you look at things, the things you look at change.' Wayne Dyer

It took me three days to get to Vienna and I was extremely excited. I managed to track them down and spent an evening in one of their ashrams. It was there that they told me about the guru coming to Vienna in a few weeks and I wanted to meet her. I stayed in the ashram for a few days and learned and practised meditation with the devotees who lived there.

On the 4th October, one day before my twenty-first birthday, I had my first drug free day. I left Salzburg and moved to Vienna and moved into the ashram.

I seemed to progress quite well, and what really amazed me was that, within a few weeks of practicing meditation, I was able to ditch my addictions – all of them. I was able to stop drugs, and I felt that I arrived in a place of serenity and balance, which I had been seeking since I was very young. I had fun, I felt I was one person again and didn't have to pretend anymore for anyone and I belonged. I found meaning, I found purpose, and I found my tribe. I found 'my people'.

It took some time before I realised it, but I became obsessed with the idea of becoming the 'super yogi', and you could almost say that one addiction was replaced with another.

The group's philosophy was very simple: if you work on yourself – if you meditate every day and clear your chakras – you will get to a higher level of awareness and be able to see who you really are; and won't be anymore fooled by the illusion of your own ego or your own conditionings and ultimately achieve enlightenment. It sounds simple enough.

The reality was slightly different. I spent every morning and every evening meditating. I spent at least one weekend almost every month in a larger community, or sangam. I lived in an ashram, and every year from that year on – for the next twelve years – I flew to India for four to six weeks to travel round with the group and our guru, meditate, and explore my deeper meaning.

It was on my second trip to India that I took advantage of a very special offer the group made available to the committed devotee: the opportunity to have an arranged marriage. To not choose your own partner but let the guru and her advisers pick someone for you to spend your life with. After all my failed relationships and my obsession with sexuality in my early teens that had resulted in such an unholy and unhappy existence, I gladly took the opportunity to let my guru choose for me. It was the ultimate test of surrender of your ego and for the 'aspiring super yogi' a challenge I could not forego. I was pretty nervous, but told myself that, whatever my mind would tell me on the day when presented with my future wife, it would just be an illusion and I would not question my guru's choice. A very few months later, that illusion turned into reality when I was married to an English girl.

My mum had freaked out when I joined the 'cult' as she called it, even when I tried to explain to her how it saved me from drug addiction; an addiction she wasn't aware of! But when I came back

Chapter 5

married from India, we stopped talking. It wasn't until my son Siddhartha was born before we started to talk again.

Life wasn't easy because I had no skills. Life wasn't easy because I lived in ashrams with my new wife and we didn't get on that well. I was messing around at uni anyway, so I decided to stop my studies. Besides, being married, I needed to make some money. I meditated every day and asked my guru for guidance, answers and money. But before the answers came, I had to go out there and earn a living.

I still loved and wrote music, and the group and the new found ideals were fertile ground for inspiration. But there was no way I knew how to make money with that. I couldn't get a job either, so I founded my first company. It was a marketing company because I loved marketing – at least, the idea of it – and I had learned little bits of it at school and at uni.

Needless to say, we were broke; in fact we were in massive debt. We were a young couple with no money, living in an ashram in one room, which wasn't perfect breeding ground for happiness and contentment. After three years I was disillusioned with the group, with my relationship, and I wanted out.

I thought that I could just leave the group, dissolve my marriage and start anew. My best cowardly plan to achieve this was to find a girlfriend that would 'solve' the situation. I am actually embarrassed to write about this, and I almost left it out of the book, but I promised myself to give a truthful account of the extent of my incapability to make mature emotional decisions at that time. I started seeing a girl but before anything really happened I was found out and the ashram leader called me for a meeting.

I wasn't prepared for what was to come. I thought they'd kick me out, as the moral code of the group was very clear. To my surprise they decided to forgive me and give me one more chance! In a last desperate attempt to fix my marriage, my wife and I decided to go to India one more time to see if we could fix our relationship. We borrowed the money and went. We didn't resolve anything, we were still as stuck as before, both pretending to be someone we weren't, eager to hold on to our illusion of being yogis.

When I arrived back in Vienna I started to feel strange, I had fever and pain in my whole body. I had been so well conditioned that I immediately thought it was God's punishment for me wanting to leave the group and having had impure thoughts about this girl. One of my brothers in the ashram assisted me with giving me cold baths and showers to 'get rid of the negativity'. When my fever got higher and the pain got worse, I also noticed my skin changing and my eyes going yellow.

I had contracted hepatitis in India and had to be rushed to hospital. I spent three weeks in hospital and my liver, damaged from all the years of drug abuse anyway, got another pounding battling with the infection. My wife also starting feeling sick but wasn't yellow, so we didn't know what was wrong with her. She was also rushed to hospital and they were stabbing in the dark about her condition. They almost operated on her stomach 'just to have a look' but finally connected the two stories and also diagnosed her with hepatitis and found to our surprise that she was – pregnant. There was a real danger for the baby with Clare having a liver infection and I was in shock anyway, because I didn't want to have kids at this stage at all.

Chapter 5

I was broke, in crisis in the group, in crises with myself and my wife, when later this year, in 1992, my son was born at home. He was a quite a small child, most likely because of his mother's liver infection in the early stage of her pregnancy. As the group's tradition suggested, our guru gave him an Indian name, Siddhartha.

My refuge was the music I wrote and I worked with a few yogis in a band. Through a stroke of luck we managed to get two of our songs published on a sampler of many bands. The radio stations picked it up, and suddenly my song was played on the radio; a brief moment of excitement; a brief moment of vision of how life could be. And when I signed my record contract in 1994, I thought I had it made.

Unfortunately I was screwed by the record company, and I ended up taking a loan of £4,000 to pay for the recording and printing of the CDs, which got me even further into debt. I earned less than £500 a month back then. I was optimistic though, that I could make my money back, as my song 'She Does It All', a song dedicated to our guru, was entering the charts. We were in a race against time to get the CDs into the shops. We had a window of opportunity, while people called the station and requested the song. They wanted to buy it, but couldn't. It drove me nuts! The radio stations stopped playing the song literally the week the record was finally available. I carried the thousands of CDs with me for years and moved them from one house to the next, until in 2007, I finally threw them out.

My decision was made though; I wanted to move to England, the home of all good pop music; the hub of the european music industry. I was ready to take on the world, and, without knowing anyone, in debt and without any proper skills, I packed up my family and my guitar and moved to the UK.

My Journey & The Machine

Chapter 6

Living On An Island

'Every man builds his world in his own image. He has the power to choose, but no power to escape the necessity of choice.' Ayn Rand

Life got worse, not better, as living in the UK as a foreigner with no skills and a young family wasn't easy. And singing my songs with an Austrian accent wasn't too great either. I started to play in pubs and clubs and was hoping to get discovered. My 'success' from Austria didn't mean much here in the UK.

Within six months I had not made a penny from my music and our situation was pretty drastic. The only skill I had acquired in Austria was a bit of self-taught computers, so I try to get work as a graphic designer and I managed to scrape by. Two years later, financially in a big mess, my self esteem had hit rock bottom. With our relationship strained as it was, and with us barely hanging on, my daughter Aparna was born in May '96.

I was still meditating every day, now in an English ashram, living with people I had never met before; not knowing how to survive; not feeling proud of myself; not feeling that I would fulfil the role of a man, truly, and definitely without a plan to change my fate.

At that time I was still freelancing as a graphic designer, when one day, one the companies that hired me regularly, offered me a

57

full time job. Believe me, a fixed job with regular income sounded as sweet as can be, and I gladly accepted.

My boss' name was Brent Curless, a friend and inspiration to me this day. Brent was a strong and powerful leader and as I had no car after a write-off accident a few months earlier, he picked me up every morning and we drove to work together. He had a BMW, owned a business, had property and spoke of self development. I had no car, no business, no property and generally no clue. I was intrigued. How could I be more like him and less like me? He shared his story and philosophy with me and I shared mine. He saw and encouraged a part of me that I hardly remembered and that I had almost forgotten.

So soon I started to read books about self-development outside the meditation's usual realms, something that was frowned upon in the group. In my desperate attempt to make money, I joined a multi-level marketing company called Euphony. It was through the weekly opportunity meetings that I was introduced to the knowledge and the philosophy of Jim Rohn; that changed everything. I have to thank Jim, and sadly will never be able to do so in person, as he passed away in December of 2009. But Jim's philosophy gave me hope again. In his simple wisdom he stated: 'You're not a tree. You can change.' And change I did. I started to believe that I could change everything about my life. I started to believe that I could learn about money. I read books about money. I read books about business. And for the first time again after many months I was full of confidence that I could turn it all around.

I remember being broke, and I remember that what I hated most about being broke was the fact that I had no control over my life. I seemed to be stuck going to work every day into a job I hated; spending hours on the road; worrying about petrol prices going up.

Chapter 6

I remember taking £10 out of the cash machine which was our spending money. I remember having little envelopes with cash for different purposes. I remember hating holidays and birthdays and Christmas, as they just cost money. I remember hating every person that had money and hoping the washing machine wouldn't pack up.

I remember the painful realisation that I had, at age thirty one, nothing to show for, and nothing to be proud of. I remember being in a place where most things just made no sense; the relationship I was in made no sense; the religion I was in no longer made sense; the job I was in made no sense. And I just wondered where it would all go? Having more money though seemed to hold the key to fix it all.

All I had to do was learn the skill of making money and acquiring wealth.

Chapter 7

Smoke And Mirrors (and The Holy Grail)

'Happiness, that grand mistress of the ceremonies in the dance of life, impels us through all its mazes and meanderings, but leads none of us by the same route.' Charles Caleb Colton

Suddenly, it was all about the money. Suddenly I realised that focusing on spirituality for ten years of my life and neglecting the important area of finances had put me in a very vulnerable and very weak position. Multi-level marketing seemed to offer me not just an additional income, but a whole new perspective on life with unlimited potential in exchange for a little of my time. And all I had to do was follow a proven step-by-step system.

I was sold! They told me that all I needed to do was talk to people, and the rest would follow. That was the brochure! The reality was that I had to learn about this new business the way I had learned about spirituality: I studied, I bought books and I spent time. When I say I spent time, I'm talking a serious amount of time. At the end of my day job, I spent most evenings until two or three in the morning, every waking hour. Three nights out of the week I travelled to Heathrow to be at the public opportunity meetings. And the rest of my time I spent on the phone, prospecting, trying to sell people into my business. Looking back, I was alive; alive with hope. Not that I had great results, but I was just excited about the fact that I had a plan B and didn't have to rely on my job's income.

This was maybe the first time that serious cracks appeared in my relationship with my wife and also my faith in the group started to wain. I felt that I had been led astray; by no fault of the group or our guru, but mainly myself by being obsessed and narrow-minded about my life's ambitions.

Spirituality served as a great excuse to disguise the lack of success I had in the 'real world'. Being an artist as a second line of defence, I could win any argument about my poor situation, but it was an empty win. Because deep inside I knew that I was losing the battle for success, meaning and self respect.

It was all about the money now, and I can tell you that the group and my peers did not like the new me one little bit. Looking at my library today, at least fifty of the hundred or so books about becoming a millionaire were bought in the short space of a year when I started on my journey of finding out how money worked, how business worked.

As I said earlier I would highly recommend you invest in Jim Rohn's books and DVD courses. For example, 'How to Have Your Best Year Ever' is one of the best resources on life and money I have ever watched. I've taken copious notes about every aspect of his very simple and deep philosophy, which seems to be able to combine an empowering lifestyle and a good life with being wealthy; something I believed were two conflicting beliefs.

Let me say one thing about being spiritual – if you use it as an excuse not to do well in the material world, then you got to wake up. There is no reason why you can't do both! But I meet many people, and I was one of them, who, almost with arrogance, present

Chapter 7

their failures in business as a merit, or consequence of their spirituality. That is plain nonsense! Why don't you drop that belief and replace it with something more powerful like the idea of becoming an enlightened millionaire? Scary at first, it became a liberating belief for me.

As I spent more and more time outside the home and the ashram, getting up at five in the morning, and working until after midnight, I became insular and obsessed once more. A new addiction was found; the addiction of finding out how to make money. Jim Rohn said that everything was a study. 'If you want to be happy, study happiness, if you want to be wealthy, study wealth'. Wise words indeed! And study I did!

I had built my first multi-level marketing business to over 1,000 members with over 120 consultants in my team. I learned very valuable lessons on leadership and business; I remember becoming a 'Principal Consultant' and Gary Lester, a leader in the business, calling it a 'coveted' position. I had to look up what it meant, but with only a handful of us among the 30,000 consultants in the UK and with the applause in the room I knew I had achieved something special.

I would strongly encourage anyone delving into at least one MLM or Network Marketing company. Not for making money, because most of them won't make you much money, but for the training they provide on marketing, business and self development.

Although I made over £1,000 in extra income, which was a lot of money considering my circumstances, I started to have doubts in the company's direction and overnight, from raving fan and dedicated promoter, I stopped. I realised that I could not endorse or promote something I didn't believe in.

This is just one of the reasons I had to start my own company, so that I was 100% in control of what I was selling and delivering.

Chapter 8

A New Paradigm

'Most of us are willing to do more for others than we are willing to do for ourselves.' Daniel Wagner

My graphic design job at 20/20, Brent's company, paid £28,000 a year, less than £2,000 a month after tax, and I although I was grateful for a full time job at first, I felt trapped. I was good at what I did, but I was bored to death, watching the clock. I dreamed of a different life, but had no idea how to move towards it. I had two bosses, Brent who thought I was a great guy and Emlyn who thought I was a prick. I remember him once calling me into his office and asking me if I thought I had 'sunshine coming our of my ass'. I quite liked the picture, but I knew he was upset because I spent most of my day surfing the internet for opportunities, looking for ways out of my predicament and some of my co-workers told him about it.

The money I earned just didn't go anywhere, as we were still paying back debts from Austria every month. I was looking for freelance work along side my job and found a nice older couple in Windsor, friends of Brent, who paid me £20 an hour to do retouch work on images. Within a few months I had a good extra income, but it meant – yet again – working full time and spending nights and weekends making the extra required to feed my family.

65

Brent was already focusing on his property business and Emlyn seemed to get more stressed by the minute. He saw himself putting in all the work while Brent was making half the money part time. One fine day, it must have been Autumn 1999, I was called once more into Emlyn's office. Emlyn had secretly planned a coup and started his own company, taking on all the existing employees. When I say all of them I mean all of them but me. His reasoning was that I was friends with Brent and he didn't want me on the team. I guess it had to do with my ability to produce sunshine out of my rear end at will as well.

I was devastated – that wasn't good news at all, so close to Christmas. I had of course, no savings and no plan B. Coming home from work that day was hard. What would I say? But worse than that was that I felt so hopeless, as a man, husband and provider. The permanent pressure of not getting by was starting to get to me.

On a side note: I went to see Emlyn years later to tell him who glad I was that he had not taken me on, because it was the beginning of my success story and that I didn't want him to feel bad about it.

What next?

Back in Austria, before I had moved to the UK in 1995, I worked in a small design company and we published a magazine for tourists. Our revenue came from selling advertising. I thought that Windsor was the perfect place to launch a magazine like this.

I needed someone to start this venture with, so I convinced the couple I was working with in Windsor to join me. I also wanted another designer, so that I could focus on the selling. My choice, and looking back I just wondered what I was thinking, fell on the

Chapter 8

already struggling friend of mine from the yoga group, Mario. We started Wagner & Barba Associates and the future was wide open.

Unfortunately 'Riverside', the magazine, wasn't a big success. It just made enough to pay me what I earned before at Brent's, and I was working sixteen hour days again. We struggled for a year, battling low margins, high cost, late paying clients and total lack of business and marketing knowledge. It was 'no future' all over again. In December 2000 I went to see one of the few friends I had within the group, Steve. Steve was an ex drug addict like me and found salvation in the group like I did and he had an arranged marriage like me as well. While I was matched with an English girl, he was married to an Austrian girl. We both had a good whinge every time we got together, talking about how we had pulled the short straw when we were matched back in the eighties. It was a way to cope, but it was all nonsense. Blame, complain, justify. The traits of a loser! And it's not like Steve and I were great catches!

Steve had been struggling like me, working in security jobs and in graphic design, but he was also furthering himself with qualifications. When I met him in December, he told me about this new job he had as a trainer for this American software company, Novadigm (meaning new paradigm). He showed me what the software did, which went right over my head. He was extremely excited, but I what really blew me away is that he told me he was paid £40,000 a year, was flying business class and stayed in five star hotels, while 'legally' being away from his wife five days a week.

Talking about a dream job! The expanding team was looking for a German speaking trainer and Steve organised an interview in Paris, the company's headquarters.

I have to thank Steve forever for what he did for me in the next three weeks. First of all we created a CV out of nothing, and even with all the pink glasses in the world it was obvious that I was just a nice guy without a chance. I had no PC or corporate or technical experience, I pulled in my Euphony training experience as relevant and my failed businesses as proof of creativity.

The company flew me to Paris in business class, put me up in a five star hotel and went for the interview. The boss was kind but straight, he told me that he had seen better and more suited CVs, but he also told me he liked my attitude and would give me a chance to prove myself by doing a presentation for his management team in three weeks time.

Wow! Steve and I decided to blow them away by doing a live demo of the software I was to train on. Just to put this into context, this is one of the most complex software tools to manage large corporate networks based on proprietary technology. Steve worked with me over the phone to prep me. I had no PC, no idea of networks or any of what I needed to impress them and clinch the deal.

There were so many co-incidences and strokes of luck happening the next few weeks it was just amazing. I needed a PC to learn and test the software and prepare the live demo. I found an old PC in the loft, that Clare had on loan from the Open University. It was a 486 machine and I tried to run an enterprise solution on it. Somehow, with many late nights (what's new) I managed to get it going. I struggled with the concept, I struggled with the software, I definitely struggled with my self belief, and I remember two weeks in that I wanted to give up. It was because of Steve that I carried on, because I didn't want to let him down and disappoint his investment and belief in me.

Chapter 8

Steve had drawn me a map of the training room, where the different computers were I needed for the demo, and I was up all night putting final touches on my powerpoint presentation. I had never used a PC before and we are talking Windows NT 4.0! The forty five minute presentation started well, when they asked me what I was presenting on and I told them I would do a live demo of their latest software. Their eyes popped and their jaws dropped and they wanted to know how I got my hands on the $70,000 license for the server software. I wasn't prepared for that question!

Audacity, charm, determination and a little bit of luck. I got through it and Peter, the boss, asked me to come into his office after the presentation. Steve had prepped me for this conversation. Peter said that he was very impressed with my presentation skills, and that we would consider taking me on. Steve told me that I should ask for a decision there and then. I took a deep breath and told him that I needed to know now. After a few seconds of silence, Peter said: 'Alright then, you're in. You can start 1st April and your salary will be £40,000 plus benefits.'

I wanted to jump up and hug him, but showed surprising self control and thanked him for the opportunity. I called Steve straight away and told him the good news.

Clare was delighted as well, as she hated me being self employed and the only person that wasn't so pleased was Mario, my partner in Wagner & Barba Associates, which we had to wind down.

I loved my new job, I had a company car, share options, private health insurance and accumulated thousands and thousands of airline and hotel points, that would be paying for my family holidays for the next few years.

Steve trained me well and within just six weeks I was training BT engineers, then the Inland Revenue and other big companies. Although I was the least knowledgable trainer, I always got the best marks, because I connected with people and cared about them more than the software. In the next four years I trained in most European countries and in the US, Hong Kong, Singapore, South Africa and Israel. I always flew out on a Monday and returned on a Friday. People asked me, how I could bear to be away from my family, but that really wasn't a problem. I was happier away than home and finally felt I was making progress.

Although I earned a lot more money than ever before, we spent it all. We had finally moved out of the Ashram into our first house in Slough and then moved into a better area a few years later.

The entrepreneur in me couldn't be stopped and I spotted an opportunity that was to double my salary! Steve and I used training manuals that we wrote for our courses. I sourced a printing company in the UK and as we did more trainings, this small copy shop invoiced us between £4,000 and £6,000 a month. I went to my boss and asked him if he was ok if I supplied the documentation and saved the company at least 20%? He agreed and 'Technical Documentation Limited' was born. In the next two years I produced all the manuals and CDs for all trainings and billed my own employer around £5,000 a month. It did mean that when I arrived home Friday night I started the printer and by Monday morning I had to produce 10,000 to 20,000 pages, produce and pack the manuals and send them via UPS around Europe. I loved it. It allowed us to pay back our debts and I started saving some money for the first time in my life.

In February 2005, Novadigm was bought out by HP, I was suddenly part of a 160,000 people workforce (Novadigm had less

Chapter 8

than 300 employees) and with the biggest printer company in the world owning us my 'produce the manuals' deal was off the table. I lost 50% of my income overnight.

Again, I had to look for alternative income streams. The great thing about the takeover by HP though was that my role changed and I was in the UK a lot more. My job was to build a training team and I could do that from my new home office.

A new window of opportunity opened up. I was already in touch with Vanish Patel, who was running property meetings in London and now that I was able to attend their mid-week meetings, property was to be my next income model!

Chapter 9

Almost Brave Enough

'For you can do whatever you want, but remember, it is also you who has to face the consequences of what you have done.' Anon

It was Christmas 2002 when Clare took the kids to India and I stayed back in the UK. I spent Christmas with my mum and dad in Innsbruck and I stayed in my old bedroom. Like most people in Austria, my parents never moved and still live in the tower block apartment I grew up in when I was a kid till this day. So there I was, back in my bedroom, looking out the same window onto the mountains. It was snowing and I started to reminisce about my life. I had this strong feeling that I had to find closure with people I had disappointed while I was a young man.

There were in essence three girls that I had been with long enough to have meaningful deep relationships with. Patrizia, my first love, Rita, whom I tried to save from alcoholism by giving her drugs, and Brigitte, who was my girlfriend when I started meditating. Here was my simple and exciting plan. I would try to find them, spend and evening or a day with them and then make sure they are ok with how I broke up with them. I also wanted to prove how well I had done, now earning good money and having left the drugs behind. I thought I had a superior philosophy and I wanted to make sure they knew about it.

Strangely enough it was easy to seek them out and arrange to meet. I was excited and nervous. Brigitte was first. She was divorced again and lived in Salzburg, and within minutes she told me that she would have me back if I still wanted to be with her. We shared a lot, including having been part of the group and our relationship back in 1987. I was pleased that she didn't bear a grudge against me.

Next up was Rita. Rita was quite unstable even back when I was nineteen. The last twenty years had taken their toll on her. She worked as a postman, she had been abused many times since we broke up and she had seen Jesus and the Devil she told me. She also told me that she would be keen to get back to me if I wanted to be with her. I started to feel a bit uneasy, and declined. For the next few weeks, she kept calling me telling me that I couldn't just come back into her life and then disappear again. She was right and I wasn't so sure about my plan anymore.

Last though was Patrizia. I went to see her in her flat in Innsbruck, and the moment she opened the door I was totally mesmerised. I instantly and deeply fell in love with her again. Everything about her, from the smell and her clothes, to the food we ate and music we shared, reminded me of how I had felt almost twenty years ago. I came to see her every night that week and told her about my loveless relationship, my disappointment with the religious group and my quest for wealth and riches.

It was like coming home. My skin and body just relaxed and I was safe. Every night we got closer to each other, I even had a smoke, a joint, a glass of wine, all things that I hadn't touched for fifteen years since I started the meditation. I loved it. I wanted to do everything she did so that I could be closer to her. The third night she asked me to stay over and I agreed. I was fighting with

Chapter 9

myself and her invitation to sleep with her was almost impossible to resist. I didn't have physical contact with my wife for years at this point. I was determined though to not betray my wife and somehow did not have sex with Patrizia that night.

The next day I flew back to the UK and soon after Clare returned from India. It was a shock, the few days I had experienced were so different to the rest of my life.

My job brought me to Munich on a monthly basis for a week, less than a two hour drive from Innsbruck, my home town. So I went to see Patrizia every month. I loved it. I had my rental car, and stayed with her. We talked for hours, and I started to plan to leave Clare. I went to see a divorce lawyer in England and he told me very clearly that we'd all be broke if I was to divorce. The way he sneered at my 'balance sheet' got me so mad, I decided that I would do whatever it takes to make enough money so that I could get divorced and we would all be alright, at least financially.

By May this year, after about six months, Patrizia and I agreed that I should try to make my marriage work and that this wasn't our time. I was sad, very sad, but the fact that I felt the love for Patrizia made aware that I was not beyond help, that one day I could love again. With Patrizia I was myself, I was a good guy, funny, loving, confident — it is as if she brought out the best in me while my wife did almost the opposite. I was a different person at home.

For the next two years I was haunted by this decision. Wherever I went I believed I saw her. My mind and thoughts went back to the time we spent together. I had given up the possibility of happiness with her, my soul mate, because I wanted to be a good man. I wanted to make my marriage work.

I had made the choice to stick it out and not go with what I wanted, but with what I thought I ought to do.

It was hard to lose her again, for very different reasons this time, but I finally, after two long years, almost stopped thinking about her.

Chapter 10

What Do Millionaires Want?

'Do not lose hold of your dreams or aspirations. For if you do, you may still exist but you have ceased to live.' Henry David Thoreau

When I read Mark Victor Hansen's and Robert G. Allen's 'The One Minute Millionaire – the enlightened way to wealth' for the first time in 2002, it quickly became my bible and guide book for that year. I had many great 'aha' moments, and I learned about the 'four mountains of wealth'. Those of you who have heard me speak before might have seen me mention them: Business, Property, Stocks & Shares and Internet. Please pick up a copy of the book and don't be fooled by the title. It will take you longer than a minute to become a millionaire! Also – don't get the audio book, it's pants.

My wife hated the book (not that she read it) but she hated me reading it. She wanted me to further my career with the training company, get real and stop wanting to be a millionaire. 'The only people who became millionaires were the ones selling these books to fools like me', she said.

I knew though that my job was just a temporary stop gap. I was never gonna be an employee, never gonna settle for a salary! She ridiculed my attempts to become wealthy and it made me even more determined to achieve it.

Coming back to the book, one of the strategies it suggests is to find a millionaire, then find out what he (or she) wants and see if you can help them get it. Sounded like a great idea, with a few little flaws, the first one not knowing any millionaires at all!

Me and Mark Victor Hansen in London at a 'Yes!' Group meeting. I bought the book again to have him sign it. In case you're wondering why I am so thin, I just completed a eight month juice diet.

I went to see the wealthiest guy I knew, Brent Curless and interviewed him to see if there was anything I could do for him that could make us both money. I loved the interview, I learned a lot about his habits and even more about money, but I couldn't think of anything that I could add to his life or business. I was just about to cross out that section in the book as a 'done that, tried this, didn't work' category when my mum called.

She talked about Karin, my sister, and her problems since her husband had passed away the year before. And of course there were many challenges, but I was listening with my own needs, I was

Chapter 10

tuned into WII FM (the world's most popular radio station – what's in it for me!).

As my mum progressed with the story she told me that Karin was left an inheritance and needed to invest it, and that one of her school friends had become the director of a large financial institution. I went to the same school as Karin, and I also knew the guy! Mum told me that was now a millionaire! Bingo and Cha-Ching! I had my lead. I called him up and asked him for a meeting, for old times sake. He was curious what I had been up to, and I met him the next time I had to be in Munich with my job.

I had no idea what I could bring to the table, but I was ready to give it a go. I dug out my suit, shaved and tried to look convincingly successful, but I have to admit, entering his office I felt a lot smaller than I had planned. First of all the guy is 6'6", used to be one of the top athletes when he was younger and has piercing blue eyes and a very sharp mind. His office was as big as my house.

The conversation was friendly and he told me about the millions he made, how he made them and about his favourite charity. He was running courses and workshops for the top managers in the company, and he had his own philosophy about success and life. While he was telling me a story of him and some of the managers spending a weekend on a self discovery course in the mountains, he told me that he loved to sing and that he thought himself a bit of an undiscovered talent.

That was the moment my brain put together a little equation that was to become a €35,000 profit for me over the course of the year. Gregor has all the money he needs and more, but he has a favourite charity, loves to sing, has his own success philosophy and wants recognition like everybody else. On top of that he has almost 7,000 sales people in Austria, Germany and Switzerland that look up to him and that he has 'access' to.

Here is the idea. We create a CD, where Gregor writes the lyrics about his success philosophy and sings, while I write and record and produce the music. I will also take care of the graphics and we'll sell them at €10 to his sales guys. €5 will go to charity, he makes no profit (which makes him look good!) and I keep the rest!

My first ever collaboration with a millionaire. A music CD for charity back in 2003. I had my own record label 'soulfood records' and I made €35,000.

Gregor wrote some great poems and I put them to music. I met a guy in Munich who had produced some great albums for German bands. Within four months I had written and recorded seven songs, always spending the evenings and nights during my business trips to Munich.

The album was a massive success and Gregor was able to almost 'force' people to buy them. How can you resist, if your boss

Chapter 10

does an album for charity? We sold almost 7,000 copies, which not just made me around €35,000, but also helped to saves the lives of over 200 children in Africa.

Gregor also invited me to see him speak from stage and he told me that was paid up to €5,000 a day for sharing his story and success principles. I saw him, loved it and thought to myself: 'I'll have some of that!' Didn't quite know how, but at least I knew someone who did. I was proud and happy to tell Gregor that I had made £100,000 in a weekend in 2010!

In marketing and business terms this project had everything to guarantee success. A warm market (7,000 employees) a desirable and easy to deliver product (CD of how he became rich), emotional leverage (the money went to the companies nominated charity), and it also combined the skill of everyone involved. It was the first time I had money from my love of music. Not the way I had envisaged, but hey – sometimes you got to settle for what you can get!

To this day, Gregor and I meet once every year and discuss our progress and projects.

Chapter 11

The Skin I'm In

'I've done more harm by the falseness of trying to please than by the honesty of telling the truth and its consequences.'
Daniel Wagner

During these years of struggles I had developed some stomach troubles, nothing life threatening, but bad enough to make my life a bit of a misery. I had such bad reflux, that I could only sleep sitting up, and I consumed bottles worth of Gaviscon every day. I saw a doctor and he had the answer. Just a small operation to tighten the entrance to the stomach. Yeah right! You must be joking. Looking back I can't believe he didn't even ask me about my diet! I drank ten espressos a day, cans of diet coke and wasn't really aware of what good and bad food for my body really was. I also developed a skin rash on my legs, which made me very itchy. Knowing what I know now – I couldn't 'swallow' my situation anymore, I couldn't 'digest' my life and things bothered me, an 'itch' I couldn't scratch and not being happy in my 'skin', my situation.

A friend of mine told me about Tony Robbins coming to London in May 2005 and I had heard the name before. I looked him up on YouTube and was not convinced. It looked like a cult! This man was intense, full on, I was a Jim Rohn guy, more of a philosopher. I even had one of Tony's books on my shelf, but couldn't get into it when I tried reading it some years ago. I asked around and came across a few people I knew that had actually been to experience Tony's 'Unleash the Power Within'. All of them agreed that it would be totally life changing and that I simply had to go. Life changing sounded good to me, I wanted some change and if he was the man, I was going to see him. You can imagine what my meditation group thought about that. One guy even suggested that Tony was the devil and I would get possessed if I were to attend this event. Somehow that made me wanna go a lot more. I felt that I had given the meditation a good run, eighteen years, and that it was ok to explore other ways of self discovery. I was genuinely seeking meaning and purpose in my life and I was ready to try anything.

Tony Robbins in London May 2005. This weekend had maybe the most profound impact on the rest of my life.

So off I went, with the prayers of the group. I felt pretty weird as I joined a queue of hundreds of people and I was more than curious what this Tony guy was all about. The experience was incredible. I never had as much fun, energy, new knowledge and intense breakthroughs in my life ever within four days. What I

Chapter 11

learned about myself, human behaviour and psychology was just immense. I laughed, danced, partied, cried, jumped and shouted, I connected with strangers and had profound insights. The man was a genius. The whole event was a carefully choreographed and orchestrated show to achieve life change there and then. From the fire walk (cool moss, cool moss!) on the first evening, which came as a total surprise to many of us, to the Dickens process on Sunday. If my life needed changing, then I was in the right place.

Monday was health day, and was run by Joseph McClendon III. This guys was supposedly fifty years old, but with the energy and looking more like a thirty five year old. What I learned about nutrition and health in that single day changed my attitude to food and nutrition forever.

I was so pumped when I came back that I was upsetting everyone. I wanted to change everyone's attitude towards food, wanted to have 'passion' in the relationship with my wife, I went on Tony's '10 Day Challenge' and didn't stop. I was converted. I lost weight and started to have more energy. So what happened to my stomach operation? What happened to me having to sleep sitting up and the itchy skin? My stomach problems got better and so did my itchy skin. Food did make a big difference.

I lived in an Ashram and although we were twelve in our household, I can see from the songs I wrote at the time that I didn't really feel connected anymore. Jeremy and I worked on an album, that we wanted to release to a wider audience, but was mainly written for the yogis in our group. It was still years before I finally left the group, but there were some clues in the words I wrote. Weirdly enough the song 'Lonely' was one of the people's favourite songs on the album, which indicates to me that many felt and feel like me.

85

My Journey & The Machine

Here are the words: (you can hear and download this and many more songs on http://myjourneyandthemachine.com)

Lonely

(Daniel Wagner 2005)

I am lonely, here inside my skin
It's been so many years since I've opened my heart
And said: 'come on in!'

I am lonely here inside my shell
It's been too many years since anyone said:
'I know you well!'

No man is an island –
No heart is a stone
I am just a man trying all he can
To find my way home

I'm lonely inside this place
somebody help me somebody say
I haven't fallen from grace

I'm lonely I wanna throw it all away
when there is nowhere to turn and nowhere to go
what should I say?

No man is an island –
No heart is a stone
I am just a man trying all he can
To find my way home

Still makes me feel sad to this day when I listen to this song.

Chapter 11

'Harvest', the album, was released after just three days of recording and I still like it for its freshness. 'Harvest' became the yogis album of the year and our songs were played and played again around the world. I felt that playing and writing music was one of my callings, and I had finally found an expression for my words. My favourite songs on there: 'Katie's Song', 'Lonely', 'Forever Friend' and 'Harvest'.

My 2005 album 'Harvest' with Jeremy Clancy. We are currently working on our new album. Working title 'The Inevitable'.

From a financial point of view this was of course a disaster. Jeremy and I felt guilty about making money from it, and donated the profits to the group, and we even shipped them to different countries at cost so that they could make money from the album instead of us. We felt very grand and generous, but we were broke. What were we thinking?

Chapter 12

Other Mountains

'Don't wait until everything is just right. It will never be perfect... Get started now. With each step you take, you will grow stronger and stronger, more and more skilled, more and more self-confident and more and more successful.' Mark Victor Hansen

On my search for other avenues to wealth, inspired by the book 'The One Minute Millionaire', I knew there were only four avenues: a traditional business, stocks and shares – which really didn't attract me, property, and the internet. So property was next.

I started learning about property, and I met a great inspirational speaker, Vanish Patel, who taught me much about marketing and some things about property. Strangely enough, the internet was closely related to that business. I started to learn about lead generation, started to buy and sell properties, and, within a few years, managed to build a small portfolio. I didn't like the bricks and mortar side of the business, but I surely liked the deal-making, and I liked learning new stuff and speaking to small audiences at Vanish's events.

Business, I learned back then, was having a 'profitable enterprise that worked without me being there'. Now, if I used that criterion, then none of what I had created in my life until then were businesses. All of them were just jobs, be it in self-employment, or be it in employment. Euphony wasn't viable for me anymore, many other opportunities came and went, and I was still looking for the 'Holy Grail'. What would be the one thing that I could create that would use my qualities, give me the lifestyle I want, and buy me back the time that I so carelessly spent? I was prepared to work hard, no doubt about that.

I was a man of no hobbies. I was a man of no leisure, because all I did was try to learn about making money in different ways. As you might guess, learning also required some investment of money. In simple terms, the little money I did make from these opportunities was quickly spent back on the next level course or the next level acquisition of a new product or service.

I was a little bit computer-literate, so the internet seemed to be a logical next move for me. The combination of my knowledge from property and the internet soon became my next addiction. A gentleman by the name of Parmdeep Vadesha, who has built a fantastic name for himself in the property and information marketing industry, helped me to interview twelve of his best friends, all of them successful in property. Because of my background in spirituality and meditation, I said to him that I thought that it would be more interesting looking at their habits and their mindset than it was looking at their actual doings to create deals. One of the people I interviewed was Ranjan Bhattacharya, who became a friend and is a business partner to this day.

The product 'Property Habits' was released in 2005, and although I didn't know how we made money, we did! That was an enormous breakthrough. If you've ever started a business, then you can relate to the fact that the first dollar, the first successful sale, is a massive inspiration and builds trust in your own ability and the business model you have chosen. After the initial excitement of 'Property Habits', the money stopped. I had a product, I had a

Chapter 12

'Conversion Environment', but after Parmdeep's mailing to his list which gave us the initial boost of sales, we had no more traffic coming and I didn't have a clue what to do next.

Hanging out with successful people was inspiring, but it can also be a mirror held a bit too close to your face for comfort and it didn't fill my bank accounts.

I wondered if I was going round in circles, reminding me of the old days of drug addiction, where I was chasing one illusion after the other. I wondered if I was just a going round and round, or if there was a spiral upwards movement; that I was actually climbing and elevating myself to more and more knowledge, until I was finally breaking through the invisible veil – the glass ceiling – that separates failure from success and would ultimately reveal the holy grail, 'the machine'?

I surely didn't feel successful. All I felt was that I was on a journey, trying to make my mark and get ahead. As I got more entrenched into those wealth-seeking opportunities, from property to MLM and the internet, I discovered that people liked to hear me and my small success stories, they liked to see me on stage. I started doing short slots of ten to fifteen minutes for friends who ran their own events. I spoke and taught, of course, for free, but soon heard and learned about an industry called 'public selling', which is, selling from stage.

I wondered if that could be my calling? I had run meditation meetings for fifteen years and loved doing them; I used to be on stage as a musician, and I loved doing that. So maybe being on stage and teaching about money and helping people, was my avenue to fulfilment, meaning and the wealth I was seeking?

The discovery of the industry and possibility of public selling, was a breakthrough for me. I looked around and I learned from the best in the industry. I went on courses, I read the books, and I was given the opportunity to speak on small stages in front of small groups and I practiced as much as I could to get better.

At the end of seven years of trying to find the ultimate vehicle to creating my lifestyle and wealth I deserved, I was still broke, living from paycheque to paycheque. I had learned a lot, and knew what businesses were. I learned from Ranjan how to operate a business properly, but I had not done it yet. And as Roger Hamilton simply says, in his amazing wisdom, 'to know, and not to do, is not to know'. At this point, I knew the stuff, but I hadn't done it yet. Breaking through the next barrier was a big step, and I was afraid that it would fail again.

I started to fear that is might never happen.

Chapter 13

Onwards And Upwards

'The major reason for setting a goal is for what it makes of you to accomplish it. What it makes of you will always be the far greater value than what you get.' Jim Rohn

To sum up the last five years of my life in just a few pages seems almost impossible, because so much happened. It seems like time has sped up. It seems like more and more things happened faster, as though stretching my comfort zone has created a larger and stronger vessel able to hold and contain more precious life enhancing nectar.

The next few chapters will focus on how I fell in love with marketing and sketches out my personal and business journey, with milestones marking breakthroughs on my way to build the 'machine'.

Right now I am sitting in Starbucks in Ascot, sipping my single shot tall Americano with one ice cube (so I can drink it straight away – I love instant) to the calming sounds of coffee grinders and Arabian music. It's Tuesday morning 10am and I love where I am today. Only two years ago I gave up my full time job with HP, my life controlled and dictated by senseless tasks (at least I didn't see the point). Today I do what I want. I have the lifestyle of a millionaire, or even better than many millionaires I know. In fact, I remember distinctly last year, when I lived in Cyprus amongst empty villas owned by millionaires, who were back in their respective home countries working while I was there 'full time' enjoying the life of a marketer, having an automated income machine that I could operate and maintain from anywhere in the world.

Let's go back to 2005, almost six years ago, when I created my first ever information product, 'Property Habits'. I worked with Parmdeep Vadesha, and we had a simple deal. I was to interview twelve of his property investor friends and he would offer the product to his list and we'd split the profit. I like it when a business deal fits on the back of a postage stamp. It was the first time I was introduced to autoresponder technology, and I remember just being totally blown away by the fact that Deep was able to send hundreds of thousands of messages personalised to his prospects and customers for pennies! I had no clue how to get the product done, but with the help of Vanish Patel I was guided through. I guess the fact that I got it done said something about me and my determination.

In 2005 I didn't know that Skype existed, so I bought a call recorder from Maplin for £9.95 and cut my phone line in two and somehow patched it into my laptop with some Sellotape... a crude solution and the results were less than impressive. If you listen to the interviews today, you can hardly hear some of the experts! It taught me though that information products were immensely powerful. How come people would pay for an audio recording they could hardly hear? Because the information contained within the audio was valuable.

The intangible benefit though from creating the product was the connection with the experts and my association with them. The power of association meant that I was suddenly one of them, and I

Chapter 13

became a peer and friend and in some cases, created the foundation for long lasting business relationships. What was amazing is that within weeks of doing my first interviews, more experts wanted to get interviewed, and this is how I met Ranjan Bhattacharya, who was not on the original list drawn up by Deep.

The 'interview the expert model' is to this day a great way to get your first product done and to break into a market and get connections with the movers and shakers. Just a few months ago, Phill Turner, one of my coaching clients, created two products about 'driving traffic' using the same strategies I used back in 2005.

I learned about sales letters, guarantees and offers. We offered the product at £14.95 for shipping and handling and then charged £147 after thirty days, a strategy that I replicated in 2010 with the 'Lead Generator Masterclass' home study course launch.

'Property Habits' was a success and I banked my first £1,500 from the initial launch. I didn't know all the pieces of the puzzle involved, but I paid attention and copied what I could.

Deep didn't just put the money into my bank account, he actually gave me an envelope with £10s and £20s. Smart, as it looked a lot more than it was and I had that envelope with me to treat me and the kids for weeks to come.

So I had made my first money online, but didn't really know how I did it. I went out and applied for a merchant account and got turned down, I signed up for all the services Deep had to emulate his success. Needless to say that the tools were not even half the success! Or to put into a musical context, if you bought the same guitar and amp as Eddie van Halen, you're still not gonna sound anything like him.

The summer of 2005 was a frustrating time. I had made some money online, I was a micro celebrity in the small circle of Vanish's 'Property Networking Club' and I was proudly wearing my 'Expert' badge. A far cry from doing the cloakroom a few months before! With all that though, I sure knew that I didn't have a business yet. The 'machine' was still a dream.

The same summer we were invited by my father in law to go to Los Angeles. My wife and kids went for a month, I followed later for a couple of weeks. I could have never have dreamed of paying for the trip, but having been invited was an offer I couldn't refuse.

Deep gave me a CD full of ebooks, PDFs, audios and other resources about marketing and internet marketing, and I printed the whole lot out and started going through this stuff. From Gary Halbert's letters and Dan Kennedy's 'NOBS' newsletter to Maxwell Maltz's 'Psycho Cybernetics' and hundreds of audios from Alex Mandossian and others. On top of that I spent many hours talking with and learning from Vanish, who generously gave of his time and knowledge.

Amongst the many things I did in these days to immerse myself into this new world of marketing was to subscribe to everyone's autoresponder. One of them Corey Rudl's 'Internet Marketing Centre'. Corey tragically died in a car accident June 2nd, 2005.

His successor and right hand man, Derek Gehl, put on a conference in San Diego in August 2005 and by a stroke of luck I managed to combine my father in law's invitation with me being at this conference.

I have to admit that I was totally out of my depth and didn't understand what they were on about all weekend, but I met a few great and impressive people, including Jermaine Griggs, founder of

Chapter 13

hearandplay.com, Derek Gehl from the IMC and a guy called Tom Tate, who was a guest of honour as the result of being the winner of the 'Thirty Day Challenge' 2005.

Just one of the guys, but this 'accidental' meeting with Tom was to become one of my life changing events.

That weekend in San Diego was my first 'bootcamp experience' and I was impressed!

In fact I was so mesmerised, then when Derek was on stage delivering his final offer (I did't have a clue what he sold but loved it anyway) I must have been out of my mind and bought their $7,000 mentoring program, spending about $6,500 more than I had! I saved over $14,000 off the original price!

I had witnessed the power of a room full of excited people and I signed up almost against my will. I wish I had kept the sales letter and taken notes on the sales process. It was sweet! Even sweeter is the fact that five years later, I ran my own two day event where I sold my own $8,000 mentoring program, using many of the techniques used from that weekend. But more about that later.

A few weeks after I arrived back home in the UK, there arrived a sports bag full of products, DVDs, CDs and folders. On top of that I had this coach in the US who was scheduling calls with me! You guessed it – I was totally overwhelmed. I was also feeling very stupid for having bought this stuff without any idea what it was and how to make it work.

I panicked and wanted out. I called the company. I wanted a full refund! To their credit they gave me all my money back (phew!) and I sent all the stuff back (I had made copies of two manuals which I finally threw out two years later after they had gained dust on my shelf – stuff my friend calls 'shelf development'). My wife never found out that I had spent $7,000 on information products! (Unless she reads the book).

So the good news was that I had my money back, the bad news was that I still had no clue how to get started to finally make money online! The other good news that I could see first hand that people (like me) would spend thousands of dollars to learn this stuff from someone who knew how to make money online. I was determined to be that person.

Armed with a plan I consulted with my mentors Deep and Vanish and we came up with the idea to re-launch 'Property Habits' to the wider property investment community. Vanish's 'Property Networking Club' meeting seemed to be the perfect place.

I had seen what they did in the US so I thought to myself, 'how hard can it be?'. Simple plan and it'll be easy pickings – or, so I thought! Again, my basic lack of understanding of marketing and

Chapter 13

sales was causing my failure. We put in a lot of effort and with the help of my friends and contacts we managed to get about a hundred people in a room. I was so excited. I visualised the sales presentation, the people running to the back and surrounding me.

The presentation went well, I cracked some jokes, shared some of what was on the CDs and then came the crucial part – the pitch. I crashed and burned. I was so confused about the offer that nobody bought a single CD. I think out of pity one person bought a CD for £1!

The idea was that they could choose any CD they wanted from the set of twelve for £1 and then in thirty days we would send them the rest. People couldn't decide which one the wanted for £1 that evening, so they decided to do nothing. The whole ordering process and fulfilment was a mess. That was a great marketing lesson, but to be honest, one I could have done without at that time in my life. I needed to succeed! But as Jim Rohn so wisely remarked: 'Life doesn't respond to need, life responds to deserve' – thanks, Jim.

I had just turned thirty nine a few weeks before, and that evening, I felt further away than ever before from my goal which was to build 'the machine' and the life of my dreams. When I packed up the two hundred CDs that I thought I would sell this evening and carried them to the car, I heard a little voice in my head telling me to give up, to stop fooling myself that I could ever become anything other than a 'try-hard' and a failure.

I took my little voice's advice and for a week or two gave up. With the cold November rain and the bleakness of winter coming, I wasn't in any great mood to welcome the coming new year.

Brent Curless, in the new year, had been inspired by Vanish's property event in London, was planning his own version of the event in Old Windsor. Somehow, he asked me to speak there for a fifteen minute slot. I shared some of my story and what I had learned from it when I realised that the whole room was listening and being touched by the anecdotes I shared. One person, Dwayne Kerr, asked me when my next one day workshop would be. This cheeky fellow knew exactly that I didn't have a one day workshop, but as the question was out, I decided to ask the room by a show of hands who would be interested in a workshop if I ran one. With the majority of hands going up, something inside my smiled! I was back.

I started to plan my 'Property Mindset' workshop and four months later still hadn't progressed very much. I did heaps of research and reading and put together enough materiel for a two week course!

As this stage I worked part time as a Pizza guy for Dominos Pizza and spent every other night in my shed burning the proverbial midnight oil. Being caught in the proverbial paralysis of analysis.

I was simply afraid to to set a date and get it done.

Chapter 14

I Don't Like Dogs

'If you can look at a dog and not feel vicarious excitement and affection, you must be a cat.' Anon

Just to be sure you are not off burning this book now and tell your friends about me – 'a guy who doesn't like puppies?' It is not strictly true. I am ok with dogs! But it has been one of longest standing jokes from stage when I tell people how I made my first proper money online. I tell them I made money in a market I knew nothing about. It is, in stylistic terms, a climax: 'I don't have a dog, I know nothing about dogs, I don't even like dogs!' It is (at least in a room full of people and in the context of the story) a funny line. Let's get back how my 'love for dogs' came about.

One late evening, it was the 30th June 2006, I received a skype call from a familiar name. Tom Tate, the kind man I had shared a drink with in San Diego the previous summer. We had a nice chat back then and took a photo together, and that was it. I hadn't heard from him all year until that day.

Tom said, that I had to get myself on the 'Thirty Day Challenge'. I wanted to know why and he told me how it had changed his life when he completed it the previous year. He explained that it was a thirty day free mentoring program with a couple of guys called Frank Kern, and Ed Dale, and that it would be starting the next day. I had never heard of Frank Kern or Ed

Dale, but I liked Tom and he made me promise that I would complete the thirty days, no matter what.

I already was more than busy just trying to get by, but I did make time for the 'Thirty Day Challenge' – and it was a challenge. After my busy day of trying to survive in my job and all of the other things I already did, I added four to five hours of study to my schedule; and I mean study. There was 'homework' literally every day.

The amazing result, though – I was very determined – was that, on day seventeen of the program, I made my first dollar online. This time properly, through my own research, my own skills, and my own doing. I was absolutely delighted.

To be exact, it was $14.28 for the sale of an ebook – wait for it – about dogs. I knew nothing about dogs and it is an important point, because you can make money in a market you know nothing about. Over night I became a 'dog expert' selling dog ebooks – not my own at first, but I made money as an affiliate.

That really changed my life. I was able to drive more and more visitors to my opt-in page, I was able to build a list, and I sold them products. Not just one, but many different ones. The 'Thirty Day Challenge' was a breakthrough for me. I had built a list of over 23,000 names in the dog training within six weeks, driving traffic through Google Adwords.

During 2006 I had been helping Ranjan with his 'Monitorship Programme', recording audios and videos of all guest speakers with the prospect of putting a product together at the end of the year. In September I went to see Ranjan, my good friend and advisor in all things business and making money.

Chapter 14

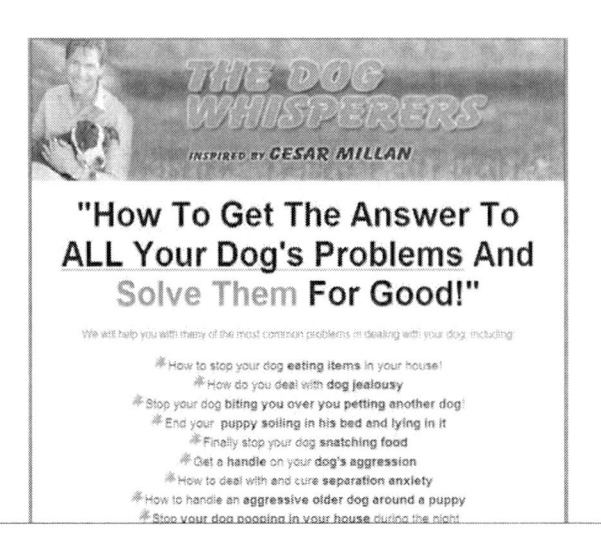

> **THE DOG WHISPERERS**
> *INSPIRED BY CESAR MILLAN*
>
> **"How To Get The Answer To ALL Your Dog's Problems And Solve Them For Good!"**
>
> We will help you with many of the most common problems in dealing with your dog, including:
>
> * How to stop your dog **eating items** in your house!
> * How do you deal with **dog jealousy**
> * Stop your dog **biting you** over you petting another dog!
> * End your puppy **soiling in his bed and lying in it**
> * Finally stop your dog **snatching food**
> * Get a handle on your **dog's aggression**
> * How to deal with and cure **separation anxiety**
> * How to handle an **aggressive older dog** around a puppy
> * Stop your dog pooping in your house during the night

The first website I made money with. I was lucky to be coached by Frank Kern and Ed Dale for free in 2006.

I told him about the dog ebooks and he just looked at me and shook his head. In his true words, he said, "This is a lot of bollocks. You should start teaching what you learned instead of selling dog ebooks." This one distinction set me on a course to where I am today.

In my quest to learn more about making money online and the journey to success, I had come across a young charismatic guy called Mark Anastasi and I attended one of his events.

It was called 'Financial Freedom and Wealth Creation', a four day event. I could only attend Saturday and Sunday as I was in a full-time job, but on Saturday morning I waited outside, early in the morning, and I told Mark about my success with the dog ebooks, and he said, "Why don't you share that with everyone in the room?"

Mark Anastasi and I at the event, just after my 'case study presentation'. I was on cloud nine, when the Mark told me that he wanted to work with me.

I worked late into the night on Saturday to prepare my presentation and on Sunday morning I did my speaking slot; my first proper speaking slot in front of eighty four people. I had fifteen minutes, and I had to give it my best shot. I loved it and luckily, a guy by the name of Mo Latin recorded that presentation which became the cornerstone of my future success.

At the end of my fifteen minute presentation I simply asked the room, "Who would like to learn what I've done?" And as every hand went up, I did my market testing in just fifteen seconds. I handed out optin forms and offered them a free tele-seminar the coming Thursday. I now knew people wanted to learn what I had mastered and I had to put an offer together fast.

Chapter 14

Ironically I had spent almost six months working on the 'Property Mindset' course and I had just agreed to run it on 7th October 2006. All I needed now was an Internet Marketing course — and fast!

I offered people a one day workshop for £147, I made some sales, and now I had just three weeks to get my first 'Internet Workshop' ready. I rolled in a guy I had met at Mark Anastasi's workshop who seemed to be quite technical who I had met Saturday morning and I was looking for another partner. The next day I enjoyed a moment of serendipitous luck.

When I was on the 'Thirty Day Challenge' back in July, I had teamed up with a guy called Saumil Patel, and we had a few brief encounters online. So I was surprised to hear from him out of the blue and he told me there would be a workshop in Old Windsor with Alan Forrest Smith and some big names from the US. Somehow Saumil had two free tickets and asked me if I wanted to go. He actually asked if anyone wanted to go with him and I was the first one to respond.

Saumil was a lot more experienced than I and during the weekend I spent with him I convinced him to run the workshop with me and we sketched out the content in one morning. We simply wanted to distill the 'Thirty Day Challenge' into a one day workshop.

This was all around my fortieth birthday (5th October for you calendar). There is some significance to this, as I had set some written goals around my fortieth birthday, including running my first workshop.

The workshop was a painful experience, with real tears from frustrated delegates. We tried to get through exercises with people who were totally inexperienced; we had a plethora of challenges with technology, but you know what? By eight o'clock that night most people had their website up and running, with an optin page and affiliate offer and an adwords campaign driving traffic to it. We had achieved an almost impossible task. I had borrowed twenty computers from my employer HP and had to build a network the night before! We had charged £147 for the day and after paying all costs I had made over £2,000 – more than in my full time job in one month. I was sold.

Word spread and I became known very quickly in the industry as 'the guy who did build an online business in a day with people in a workshop'. People loved it. They went through the pain but they came out the other end with the result.

The next workshop was in November 2006 and again a great success. Saumil and I planned out first upsell, the January bootcamp, that we offered to the October and November delegates. Out of the blue, Saumil announced that he would be returning to India after the bootcamp and he wished me good luck. It was a shock, but I had no choice but to carry on. So I was forced to run the January workshop alone.

In February 2007 I was introduced to Marcus de Maria and he invited me to speak to his graduates about my course and teach them some principles. I was rubbish, but I practiced a lot and I got better. Marcus had me back and I became a regular speaker at his three day event to teach financial literacy, the 'Wealth Workout'. Marcus now works with T Harv Eker.

I had a ball, all of 2007 I ran my workshops, soon monthly, and even two booked out sessions in the month of July!

Chapter 14

At one of Marcus' events I met Dan Bradbury, a very confident (almost cocky) young man who saw me speak and gave me some hard fact feedback. In three bullets: I was too cheap, I needed continuity and I needed an upsell. Cheers Dan!

A month later I was off to to attend Harv Eker's 'Secrets Of The Millionaire Mind' course. Another coincidence had placed Harv's course exactly at the same time as a conference I had to attend with my job. So I just stayed another weekend and they paid the ticket. Cool. I could write another book about the benefit and the breakthroughs of this course, but for the sake of this summary of events let me just say that you must learn the principles and if the courses are still available, I urge you to attend one.

I realised that running workshops every month is great fun, but I didn't have a way to scale my efforts and couldn't go global. I decided to create a home study version of my one day workshop, the 'Instant Internet Cash System' and with the help of Shamir, another guy I met online in the 'Thirty Day Challenge', I had it up and running within just a few weeks.

In summer of 2007 I wanted to learn more about public speaking and training and as I loved T Harv Eker's 'Millionaire Mind Weekend', I signed up for his 'Train The Trainer' course. I heard a lot of good about it, and literally on the weekend of my birthday in 2007 I flew off to New York to become a proper trainer and learn to sell from the stage.

Every step of the way, I applied what I had learned on my journey towards building the 'machine'. I got better at marketing, better at selling, better at creating products, but what happened next was so unexpected and big for me.

Sometimes you just don't see it coming...

Chapter 15

Free-falling...

'Do the thing you fear to do and keep on doing it... that is the quickest and surest way ever yet discovered to conquer fear.'
Dale Carnegie

Writing a journal – a habit I learned from Jim Rohn – has changed my life. Also the simple habit of writing a gratitude list, five things you are grateful for every day, has definitely improved how I feel about myself and my existence. If I read my old journals, it is more than fascinating to see what was a 'challenge' one year, is part of my 'comfort zone' the next. It is also fascinating how the universe appears to make things happen once you have decided to write down what you want.

It was one of my goals to meet some of the big gurus of Internet Marketing, so in perfect synchronicity, Jason Cohen and John Thornely organised a three day event in London in September 2007 called the 'Internet Success Bootcamp'. Because of my experience in interviewing experts (they knew about my Property Habits product) and because they were more than busy running the event, I had the privilege and pleasure to interview the speakers. From Armand Morin to Mike Filsaime, and from Kirt Christensen to Marlon Sanders, I had them all – in just one weekend. What dawned on me over the two days with these millionaires and multi-millionaires, is that they were really people like you and me, most of them nice normal guys, with the little difference that they had income producing assets in the form of web businesses, they had a 'machine'.

I am grateful to Jason and John for giving me the opportunity. If you want to check out the interviews with the guys, they are still online, just go to: GrillingTheExperts.com

On the Saturday evening, when everyone had disappeared, I went into the main room and walked on stage and I looked into the auditorium – seven hundred empty seats looking back at me and I promised myself, that one day, in the not too distant future, I would be on stage telling my story.

After the weekend I had a big row with my wife because I was 'always away, just doing what I wanted'. I didn't see it that way, for as far as I was concerned I was sacrificing my spare time to find the 'holy grail', so I felt offended and hurt. So the news of me selfishly flying off and leaving her alone with the kids once more on my birthday a few weeks later didn't go down very well at all. The carelessly chosen phrase that 'it was an opportunity not to be missed', had been much overused in our household over the past many years of struggle.

How can I sum up that moment in time? I appeared to be and was successful to a degree, but with some major flaws for true integral happiness. I hated my job, I had lost faith in my religion, I didn't love my wife and I didn't feel at home, at home. So while I was chasing the dream of ultimate happiness, I only had one ingredient half sorted.

When I arrived at the airport to fly to the US, I strolled around the shops and was found by a book. You are not reading this wrong: I was found by the book. I was not looking for anything –

Chapter 15

at least consciously, but I just had to buy this book called 'The God Delusion' by the British biologist Richard Dawkins.

I devoured the book on the plane, resulting in moments of clarity and head nodding. It was truly a revelation to me and encouraged me to make an important decision. To leave my religious group behind. The thought of it scared me and frightened me, but at the same time filled me with excitement and glee. Coincidentally I sat next to a lady who had just read the book herself and as a consequence stepped out of her religious group. Looking back I can't believe just how much fear had paralysed me for years.

I loved Harv Eker's 'Train The Trainer' course and it was even better than I had hoped for. I celebrated my birthday with the three hundred or so delegates. I enjoyed myself so much that I forgot to call my wife on my birthday! One thing that always amazed me though was how of a different person I was at these events. How people perceived me and how I saw myself. I was free, enjoyed myself, was able to connect quickly and feel alive. At home I felt a lot like an idiot, pretty useless and not capable of being much use to anyone. Could it just be the environment?

I was totally fired up from the event and saw a great future ahead for me and my training business. I head learned about how to structure an upsell and how to run a 'bookshop', Harv's name for a sales pitch. I was going to try this out at my next workshop in October. So far I had sold workshop places and then just waved my customers good bye! What a wally! I even know what they wanted and needed next. So on the plane back to London I designed my 'Digital Product Creation Secrets' workshop.

But there was one area I was not so keen on and fired up about, and it was not how to sell from stage, but how to tell my wife. Tell her that the basis of our relationship was to be taken away. When we got married in India, we vowed to bring up our kids in this religion, that our marriage and our friends and our life was to revolve around it, too. We had been together for eighteen years at this stage and twenty years meditating in the group. All our friends, our 'brothers and sisters' as we call them, were in the group, I had no social life outside it and my kids were brought up in the belief and faith of the group.

Brent, my friend and mentor, once told me that whatever you have to say, it is 'just a conversation'. And I told myself that I just had to have a 'conversation' with Clare, that was all. I wasn't to predict or fear any outcome, it was 'just a conversation'. My heart was pounding. I asked Clare to come upstairs for I had something to tell her. Even just thinking about it today still turns my stomach and gives me butterflies.

"I want to leave the group. I can't be in it any longer because I don't believe anymore in what it stands for and what we do."

Wow.

That was not just a conversation, these were poisonous words and explosive syllables. I can only remember part of what happened next, but it included Clare crying, shouting and being very upset and at one point uttering that if I wasn't interested to be in the group (the last thing that we had in common) then I might as well not be with her anymore.

As terrible as it sounds, I suddenly felt that this was what I wanted. I didn't plan it that way, I was only wanting to leave the

Chapter 15

group and what I thought to be suffocating beliefs, but suddenly I felt this rush in my head and the words came out all by themselves.

"Ok, so let's get a divorce then."

I can't guarantee that these were the exact words, but I know for sure this was the meaning.

To cut the painful events to their essence, I started sleeping on the sofa soon after that. I was getting up before anyone to leave the house and going to bed after everyone just to avoid seeing any of the family for the next six weeks or so until I had found myself a little flat.

I moved to a nearby flat on 1st December 2007.

Chapter 16

...and Soft-landing

'Don't cry because it's over. Smile because it happened.' Dr. Seuss

A few things surprised me during those first few months of living alone:

1. Only two people from the hundreds I knew from the group contacted me to see how I was or to find out what really happened – I expected more, especially after all the years I had spent with them,

2. I did not fall into an abyss of sin and meaninglessness, which was one of my big fears and predictions when I left the 'safety' of the group. I actually found that I had a kind of inner 'dharma' – a set of rules of behaviour, that served me very well,

3. I found a lightness of being that I hadn't felt since I was twenty one. I felt one again. I realised just how wrong my life had been and how much I had pretended to be someone. Exhausting stuff.

In my marketing efforts the weeks after America were amazing. I just used the formula I had learned at 'Train The Trainer', and sold 40% of my workshop students onto the £1,997 'Digital Product Creation Bootcamp', which I scheduled for January 2008. That was easy and I just wondered how much money I had left on the table in the last year by not offering an upsell. More about the workshop and my learnings later.

In November I googled my name and saw that someone from Progressive Property, a company I had never heard of before, was bidding on my name. I was familiar with this strategy, scrape some traffic by bidding on people's names and redirect them to your own customised landing page. I and many of my friends used this strategy successfully, but it bothered me and intrigued me that they were bidding on my name. I called them and spoke to the man in charge, Rob Moore. He told me that legally there was nothing I could do about it, but he would stop the campaign if I really wanted him to.

At this stage I could have reacted in a few ways. Get upset, threaten or just forget about it. But we found a fourth way: we decided to meet up and I invited him to sit in on my workshop in November and have a chat after. Rob came, stayed for the whole day and signed up for the 'Digital Product Creation Bootcamp'. Rob and I have since made over £100,000 together, have become friends and have had a lot of fun along the way. Lesson? It doesn't matter what happens, it's only important what you make of it.

After the first few weeks on my own, I started to sit down and think about what the future could bring. I was in a great position, I had an open road ahead of me, full of opportunity and unlimited potential. So to design my future, I looked back on my life to see when I had been happy and what I had loved so far. The one thing that came up again and again was Patrizia and Austria. She was what I had always wanted, since I was seventeen years old. For the last twenty four years she was the missing part, my soul mate! Now I knew what I had to do. Find her (again) and tell her! And why was I living in England anyway? I was Austrian, a mountain boy,

Chapter 16

my mother tongue was Austrian and I wanted to speak it again. I was coming home!

Thanks to the internet I tracked Patrizia down and contacted her. I told her I had left my wife and was to file for divorce, I shared that I had stepped out of the group and asked if she wanted to meet with me. She still lived in Innsbruck, was working in a hospice for the last many years and had a fifteen year old son. And yes, she was single and yes, she agreed. I decided to fly out just after Christmas to meet up with her and see what would happen. I started planning my future with her. She had arranged her birthday party on the 29th and I was very curious about how she lived and who her friends were.

Christmas I spent by myself, alone, but not lonely, by myself and happy. Because of my lack of planning I had to resort to a Lebanese restaurant for my Christmas dinner, and I still see the hummus and carrot juice in front of me when I think about it. The only other people in the restaurant seemed to be single men about my age. I could only guess their reason for being there! Before you feel sorry for me though, let me assure you that previous Christmas experiences had been worse than this.

I flew to Austria on the 26th December and met the girl that I had loved since I was seventeen. What I had felt for her was always my yardstick for what love could be. Before I knew it, we were back together. I moved in with her within a day. It was so crazy to be with someone you know so well. I – or my body – still remembered her so well. The touch and the smell and everything. I had come home. I started writing music again. I wrote ten songs or so in the next few months. My heart was restored. I felt complete.

She lived in this old house on the mountain, with a small stream running through the wild gardens, overlooking the snowy valley. The house smelled of wood fire, and every room had its own wooden stove. We cooked together, all organic and local food, we had fallen in love once again.

Coming out of my marriage, where I hadn't been sexually active for years, I was slightly nervous how things would work for me and her. And the answer is that I totally loved it – I was more than fine. I remember cracking up laughing for all the playful fun we had together, just like back when we were young, only better. I was lucky I suppose, because Patrizia had attended all kinds of courses on Tantra and sexuality and she was the expert. But most of all she made me feel so comfortable and accepted, that I felt no pressure at all. You could say it was the total opposite to the philosophy I had lived by for the last twenty years in the group. So this is what life was supposed to be like? Bring it on!

I didn't want it to stop, and I didn't want to leave and go back to the UK, but I had my 'Digital Product Creation Bootcamp' to run and so I reluctantly pulled myself away from the person that seemed to so effortlessly complete me.

The bootcamp was a great success and I had it all filmed and I created a 10 DVD set from it, which I still sell to this day.

I filed for divorce in January and was hoping for a quick and painless resolution of my marriage. Between my job (yes, I was still working full time for HP), my workshops, the kids and flying back and forth from Innsbruck, the next few months were pretty busy. I didn't regret leaving my wife and stepping out of the group for a single day, but I knew that I couldn't take this step without

Chapter 16

hurting people. There are times in your life though, when you have to make audacious choices.

Everyday Patrizia and I spent hours skyping, texting, speaking, and every month I would fly to Austria for a week or ten days of very intense togetherness. It was perfect. The only thing that started to wear me down was the fact that we were not together all the time. I started to hate the time away from her. Nothing could replace being together. I also started to get involved and helped her in her business, she was running workshops on dealing with grief, and also helped her with her financial situation. This part of our relationship I didn't enjoy.

Patrizia couldn't have kids anymore, she was already in her menopause, and we were talking about how sad it was that we couldn't have a baby together. I thought I was totally up for it. She didn't have her period for over three years, when suddenly, in April, she told me that she had her period back and that we could try for a baby if I wanted. I couldn't believe what I heard! Her doctor said that because of the intensity of our relationship her body made an exception and was ready once more to have a baby, something that happens once in ten thousand women. I should have been happy!

What was weird for me though is, that words are cheap and the fact that I knew she couldn't have kids made the whole conversation about kids romantic with a touch of bittersweet melancholy. Now that she actually could have them, I wasn't so sure and my 'left brain' started to kick in. 'How old will she be when the kid grows up? Maybe it's a bit early, we are only going out for a few months. Where will we live?' Patrizia doesn't speak much English and still had her son to look after, so the UK was out of the question and I suddenly 'loved' the UK again, and moving to Innsbruck was looking more like a sacrifice than an aspiration.

I was surprised by my own emotional landscape and it brought up the big topic of 'rebound'. I just had stepped out of a marriage of almost twenty years, maybe this was all just some form of extreme rebound?

A few weeks later, in London, I met Paul Fuggle, and we discussed divorces. I shared, he laughed and told me it would take the best part of three years before he thought I could have any 'proper' relationship and I shouldn't take it so serious and have a good time. Somehow all he said made sense. I also wanted to work on my little business and build the 'machine', and living in Innsbruck would make that a lot harder.

The next time I was in Innsbruck we had a very open talk about the future of our relationship. We did some exercises about vision, first individually, then as a couple. We spend days trying to work on a plan that would suit and fulfil both of us. Sadly, we realised that although we loved being together and although we were in love, we just had different futures ahead of us for now...

Chapter 17

Confused Sometimes Am I

'Confusion now hath made his masterpiece!' William Shakespeare

Back in the UK, things were good. I had my decree nisi, the first step towards the finalisation of the divorce on the 1st April and I was running my workshops and getting my life sorted. I loved my new found freedom and even started to make friends outside the group. In particular Shamir Rele and Urmil Patel.

Spring was in the air and life was good. That Patrizia and I couldn't define or design a future together didn't bother me that much, I just loved seeing her. But I missed her for the rest of the month, three long weeks.

I had arranged for Urmil and Sham to come over to Amersham for some Thai one evening, and we wanted to discuss possible projects together. I felt like I really needed a haircut and a shave. I had this phase where I thought I should grow a beard, partly because my wife used to hate beards. Judge for yourself, but I don't think so! (Picture on the next page)

The shop I always went to since I moved to Amersham was a very average barber, with one totally not so average hairdresser, Monique. She was very distant and almost cold, not into small talk and mindless chatter. Her green eyes and black hair citing mystery, all I knew about her was that she wasn't English and that she loved photography. I had tried to flirt with her for years, but I felt distinctly unappreciated and discouraged every time I tried. I got one smile out of her some months before when I bought a book of Yann Arthus Bertrand, 'The Earth from the Air', in Singapore and presented it to her at my last visit.

This is how I went to see Monique. The hairdresser was about to close but I could demonstrate that it was indeed, an emergency.

She was a lot younger than me, and I knew she smoked, I could smell it on her. I sat there staring at her cutting my hair and trimming my beard, checking her out and finally asking her if she wanted to have dinner that evening with a couple of friends.

She said she'd let me know and we exchanged phone numbers. At ten to eight, just before I met my Sham and Urmil, she agreed. We had a great night out, she was funny, and very sexy. She drank, she smoked, she cursed, I loved it! She was so different from anything I had experienced in the last twenty years.

Chapter 17

We became friends, and because she lived just down the road from me and I had lots of spare time, I spent almost every day with her. Picked her up after work, saw her in the morning before she was off to work. I was so wanting to look after her, it was unreal. She is a very private girl, and as I got to know her better I really appreciated her honesty and friendship. She listened to countless hours of me going on about the divorce, the group, Patrizia, everything. She grew on me, and I know that I grew on her. I was funny, loyal, kind, generous and supportive – we were great mates. There were some, very rare moments, when we got close and connected deeply, but because they were so rare, I guess I paid them a disproportionate amount of attention.

I sometimes stayed over and we shared her bed. I promised myself that I would tell Patrizia whatever happened, but I understand that Patrizia didn't really appreciate my honesty.

With Monica (I started calling her by her real name) so close and Patrizia so far away, I started to think it was maybe better to go out with Monica. To be honest, I wasn't sure what was going on with me, I changed my mind every bloody day, I wanted them both and I told myself that I was entitled to it. With Paul's advice still ringing in my ear, I told Patrizia in our next meeting in Innsbruck that I wanted to enjoy the summer with her and then move back to England.

I know how this reads. Confused? You will be, because this is just the beginning of the rope I spun to hang myself. Monica and I spend every day together now, I started drinking alcohol and did outrageous things like watch mindless television with her and ate take away food. I had not watched TV for years and I fought at home to ban it, I regarded it as a waste of time and asked instead for the kids to read self development books.

So I felt like a rebel and alleviated myself from the pressure of making every hour of every day serve a greater purpose – learning how to build the machine.

We went for walks, drives and chilled at her place. We went to parks and gardens to take photos. I loved to see her work, she is incredibly talented. I think I can say that, because I used to be told that I was good at photography, but when we both took shots, mine looked like a monkey had taken them with an etch-a-sketch.

I told Monica that I had fallen in love with her about June time, not that she didn't know, but I told her that I would spend the summer in Austria and then come back for her so that we could finally live together. Just before I left for Austria, Monica took a few photos of me by the lake one evening.

Monica's portrait of me by the lake. Happy memories of newfound freedom

Chapter 17

Back in Austria, Patrizia and I were planting potatoes and baking our own bread, and I was settling in for summer. We had some plans, including a caravan holiday to Croatia and other little bits.

An unexpected email in July opened the doors to an opportunity I could not turn down. Mike Chantry, who had heard me speak at Marcus de Maria's event, told me about a speaking opportunity for trainers of Whitney, back then on of the biggest wealth educators in the UK. Their keynote speaker on Internet Marketing had canceled on them, and I had to make a decision immediately. I was on the plane back to the UK and wowed the eighty trainers with a great demo and tons of knowledge. I sold about £20,000 worth of courses and the manager, Ian, asked me to come back in October and teased me with the possibility of speaking on the big stage in January at their gala event.

That night, instead of going home, I went to see Monica. She had a visit from a friend who had moved to Spain some time ago, and she told us of her life in the sunshine. I guess I was jealous and also felt my ego challenged, because I was supposed to be the cool guy with his internet marketing business. So I don't know why, but I told Monica that her and I could move to Spain in Autumn, packing it all in and live in the sunshine, as soon as I was back from Austria.

Back in Austria, I didn't tell Patrizia about the promise I had made. I just wanted to enjoy the summer, without consequences. I should have know that there is no decision without consequences.

About a week later, Patrizia and I had a most magical day, where we both were like on acid, but without the drugs. It was just unreal. In fact, it felt so amazing, that I thought to myself that this was even better than being with Monica. I know! Confused? I was.

The very next day, I was working on an email to go out to my list, Monica skyped me from work. She never skyped, we always emailed, and she wasn't a person of many words when she wrote. But in this skype message she told me that she had fallen in love and couldn't wait to be with me when I came back after the summer. It drove me nuts. I was waiting for this message for weeks, but now it came at a moment in time when I was so sure about Patrizia. So, in a split decision, and I remember feeling all proud about what a stand-up guy I was, I told Monica that I would stay with Patrizia and that I was sorry I had promised her to move to Spain in Autumn.

Skype went dead. I felt bad. The next day I received the longest email ever from Monica, it was truthful, clear, to the point and very, very sad. I had been so focused on maximising my experience of the new found freedom, that I was unaware of the pain I was causing people who cared about me in my quest.

One of the things I remember clearly from her message was, that 'I had to be careful when I was using words, as they created desires and visions of a future for people. I couldn't just use them to achieve the emotional result I wanted in that moment.'

The next week I decided to go on a three week fast.

Chapter 18

The Fast And The Furious

'Even a happy life cannot be without a measure of darkness, and the word happy would lose its meaning if it were not balanced by sadness.' Carl Jung

I wanted to lose weight anyway, so it seemed to be the right thing to do at a time when I wanted to 'cleanse' myself. I also hoped that fasting would help me get clarity of mind. I read a lot about fasting and the great benefits, so I looked into the various options I had. I found an Austrian doctor by the name of F X Mayr, who had pioneered a technique whereby you cleanse your digestive system under supervision of a doctor. The weight loss is a given, considering you only drink water (one litre per twenty kilograms of body weight), take some bitter salt in the morning and some alkaline powder in the day. I was coming up for my 42nd birthday in October, so I thought it's a great time to get fit, lose some weight and change some habits.

I always believed in the power of seven, so forty two was a multiple of seven and I had experienced pretty much big life changes every seven years. I am not the only one advocating this theory, and it seems to be backed by some scientific biological data as well.

During my fast, I recorded videos almost every day, and you can see them on http://myjourneyandthemachine.com, but here are

My Journey & The Machine

some snapshots of 'Day 1' and 'Day 21'. Don't do this alone at home. This is serious stuff. But it sure fits my nature and personality, who likes to have instant intense experiences.

FX Mayr Day 1

FX Mayr Day 21

A picture they say, says more than a thousand words. I lost 26 pounds in 22 days and felt great (and a bit hungry). Watch my complete 'fast and furious' fasting diary at http://myjourneyandthemachine.com

Chapter 18

I convinced Patrizia to join my on my fast and we enjoyed a great summer together and saved a lot of money on the food bill! And with the end of summer came the end of our relationship. Patrizia said she didn't understand why we had to break up, and frankly, neither did I. But I was determined to get Monica back, no matter what I had to do.

On a request from Patrizia I attended a two day workshop in Switzerland. Its purpose was to come to terms with your own grieving. It was part of Patrizia's work in the hospice, and I did it as a favour for her. I thought as no one close to me had died ever, what would I grieve about? To my surprise I was crying my eyes out and saw myself being angry and furious about sad moments of my life I had pushed far, far away and didn't want to face. The process took us through the journey of our lives, identifying 'bumps' in the road that didn't quite go the way we wanted.

The workshop leaders were great and we explored all the things that were sad in our lives. My moments of sadness had to do with my dad, who wasn't the hero I wanted him to be, with my 'not being truthful to myself' and 'standing up for what I knew was right' and of course, the failed marriage. I had enough to cry about, even if no one close to me had died! What I really took away from the course was that every emotion had its right to be, it was futile to just chase and aim for happiness. I also learned how important it was to affirm the truth. To acknowledge what really was and letting go of phantasies of our life. What a relieve.

So this was perfect timing as I had to tell Patrizia the next day that we would break it off. We both agreed that it would be best to just stop communicating, however painful it may be. It was harder than I thought, and I don't know how she coped, as we had such an intense nine months together and she didn't want me to leave.

When I arrived back in the UK I went straight to see Monica. I told her that I had now left Patrizia and that I was ready for her and me to get together. Truth be told, the moment was gone. I was trying hard to get her trust back, but some things you just can't fix once they are broken.

Patrizia did contact me and asked me if I could imagine just coming for sexual encounters, with NSA (no strings attached). I wasn't sure, but as things didn't work out that well with Monica, I thought it might be a good idea. I flew off to Austria twice to see Patrizia, but very soon realised that I could not do that and neither could she. It was wrong, plain wrong. There was no context and no meaning to it.

I was lonely again, pursuing Monica who was also lonely. Moments of closeness came and went, but there was no substance for the sparks to turn into a fire.

I had in the meantime moved out of my little flat and moved into a flat I owned from my property days that was to be mine after the divorce. I had no furniture, just three desks with computers and a blowup bed from Tesco's with an attached sleeping bag.

I wanted to spend my birthday with Monica and invited her to my place. I remember when she came in and simply asked: 'Where can I sit? You got no furniture.' I didn't even notice.

In business terms, even with my life upside down and the wrong way round, I had a great few months that autumn. I decided to join Dan Bradbury's Platinum Mastermind, which became the model for my own Platinum group in 2009, and I ran my first own hundred and twenty people event in Heathrow, copying as much as I could from Dan. My investment in Dan's group was steep even at

Chapter 18

my income level, and I promised that I will make my money back quickly. That it would be within just a month surprised even Dan.

I know that some of the coaching groups out there look like a right rip off and you wonder why you would want to join any of them, but I can promise you that being in a group of like minded people at the right time in your business will pay off big time. Make sure you check them out, speak to the guys who are on them, not just the guys who run them and commit. And if they're 'expensive', you'll work harder.

In October, a consultant that I was introduced by Rob Moore, came round looked at my business. £500 later he told me I didn't have a business. I had no tracking, no numbers, no idea. It was only at this late stage that I started to use google analytics and started to measure and track what was happening out there on all my websites I had so vigorously built.

Around my 42nd birthday I spend a day in the park with Ric Bacon, my friend and awesome photographer. The cover of this book is just one of the shots he took that wonderful autumn day. Ric – thanks and thanks again, mate!

In October, I had completed another successful session for Whitney, my 'last test' and Ian confirmed that I would be a keynote speaker alongside James Caan on their stage at the end of January 2009. That was a major breakthrough! As I was looking at getting more exposure, sharing a stage with someone like James can only be a good thing.

Dan Bradbury told me to get 'continuity income' in my business, so in December I flew over Tom Tate from the US to help me design my membership site, which I was going to launch in January 2009 after the big speaking gig. It was a lot of work and I wasted many hours and lots of money, mainly not being clear what I wanted. I suppose it was my first time. If I had to do the same today I could do it a lot quicker and a lot cheaper.

In my pursuit to get Monica to spend more time with me and hopefully like me I started to offer her presents and paid things and made myself useful in that way. I bought her a telly for her birthday and other things when I could. My plan was to get a big flat and then she could move in with me. This was about the same time my son had a warning to get kicked out of school because of his low attendance rate. Clare and I agreed that he could move in with me and it was the perfect reason to get a flat in Amersham.

Me and my son finally moved in just before Christmas and I was looking forward to spending it with Monica and get ready for 2009.

If you read this book from the beginning, then you know what happened next...

Chapter 19

One Of These Days

'You can't always get what you want. But if you try sometimes you might find – You get what you need.' The Rolling Stones

It's the 25th of December, 2008, and it's four o'clock in the afternoon. I'm taking a photo of myself and, looking at the photo, I look terrible. And you know what? I feel it as well. How did I end up here? My life was supposed to be perfect; I was a speaker on stage, I was highly paid, and people were seeing at me as a role model. My story was supposed to inspire everyone else to follow in my footsteps. From where I stand today, I wouldn't wish anyone to feel like I do today. Alone, rejected, misunderstood, without direction or purpose. I worked hard and made sacrifices to get here, was it all in vain? I had promised myself to not spend another Christmas alone, but like other promises I had made to myself before, this one was broken, too. So how did I end up at this place of utter despair?

Let me just rewind a few months. All summer I was trying to go out with Monica, a girl I had fancied for many years. And we had one magical day and I forever wanted to recreate this one day – without success. Monica had been my hairdresser for many years, and had been my fantasy for so long that it wasn't even real. So I pursued her for months; I did whatever I could. I courted her, and I was the nicest guy. Brought her coffee in the mornings, picked her up for lunch, spent every evening with her and many times the night. As a friendship goes, it was great, but I was fixated with making it something else.

You see, after twenty years in my religious group to go out or even get to know a girl who drank, swore, smoked and was sexy was such an incredibly exciting thing – I was mesmerised and hypnotised. Like a moth to a flame. I didn't let go, it was an effort, I admit that, but finally, towards the end of the October, she agreed to go out with me. And why is this relevant? Because I pushed so hard. And in a way, deep inside, I knew she wasn't the one, but I was attracted by how she looked and how she behaved and how she stood out from the rest. And in a way it was the chase. I understand, looking back, that all I wanted was to win; all I wanted was to have that success, that boost for my battered ego and self confidence. It wasn't about a 'relationship' at all. I didn't actually have a clue how to have a relationship.

So autumn was a great time. I felt I was getting closer to the prize. I felt I was getting closer to my goal. And as I pushed, and as I forced myself and forced her into situations and the life that I thought I wanted to lead with her, I came to the realisation that, deep inside, my soul was torn. I felt extremely insecure around her and permanently waited for bad news to happen.

I cried; I hadn't cried for years. I cried because I was lonely. I cried because I was disillusioned. I cried because I felt that I had betrayed myself. I don't believe in soul, as such, but I felt that I had 'sold my soul'. I had given up who I was to achieve something that I thought people wanted me to achieve. I felt I acted on outside pressure. Whose pressure was this?

So how did I end up, on Christmas day, totally in pieces? Leading up to Christmas, I had just rented an expensive penthouse

Chapter 19

flat for me and my son, but with the prospect of having Monica move in with me. It gave me a bit of a stomach ache to spend so much money on living accommodation because I'd always been very careful with money, especially when it had to do with anything for myself. I'm a generous guy I think, but spending on myself was always difficult.

So I moved into this amazing place. It was big with many empty rooms. I had no furniture, so I went out and I bought what I thought she would love. And I thought, "If I make this place right, she'll move in with me". Everything was set: the big leather furniture, I bought a big plasma TV. I never had one before, but I thought, "That looks good". I bought a new car. You know, I had some money, so I thought, "Hey, let's use it. Let's impress someone".

And it worked, to a degree. I felt in my gut that something was wrong, but I just ignored that little voice. I had chosen to let myself be guided by greed and lust more than by my sixth sense guiding me towards my well-being. Many times I was suspicious that something was going on, but finally, on that day, on the day before Christmas, on Christmas Eve, things really blew up.

I haven't mentioned that it was my second Christmas without my family after the divorce, and I had spent my first Christmas alone in London in a Lebanese Restaurant eating carrot soup. Not my favourite memory.

On Christmas Eve in the afternoon, she was expected to come round and we were meant to spend the most beautiful, romantic Christmas together. (Monica as a Czech and me being Austrian means we celebrate Christmas Eve). She didn't turn up at the agreed time. So, after hours of deliberating and being worried, I finally drove down to her flat, and as I arrived I had the shock of my life. Looking up, I saw her in the arms of another guy; she in tears, he talking at her. I didn't know what to do. She hadn't noticed me yet, so I was just hiding; watching. I didn't know what had happened, but I did know something had just gone terribly wrong. I felt like a coward, sneaking back to my car and driving away. My heart was aching and my mind was racing.

I went back to the flat and waited for her for an hour, or maybe two. I had the craziest thoughts and my imagination played total havoc with me. Then I drove to her house again, at this point, knocking at her door, trying to confront her. I was shaken, I was in tears, I was angry. I had realised that I had just lost something that I thought I owned. I lost something I thought was really important to me. Mainly, what I had lost, though, was a distraction from myself. And mainly I was afraid to be alone – again.

As you might guess, she wasn't spending Christmas with me after all. So that evening when I was alone in this big flat, with everything laid out for Christmas, the food bought and uncooked, the alcohol in the fridge. I didn't drink. I hadn't consumed alcohol for twenty years before that night. Well – that changed – I drank a whole bottle of vodka, enriched with a four pack of Red Bull. I couldn't sleep that night. I wrote my Christmas story, five thousand words of coming to terms with my situation. Digging deep to understand why and how this happened. Needless to say I spent half the night on the toilet, just wanting to die. I didn't quite know what had hit me. Wasn't I supposed to be successful? Wasn't I supposed to be happy? Didn't I have the life I always wanted? Not quite. Shouldn't I know better? Apparently not.

Around lunch time the next day – I drove down to her house again. I wanted to really clear the situation up. I felt in pain – not

Chapter 19

just from what I'd done to myself the night before, but the emotional pain of disappointment and disillusionment; the emotional pain of loneliness; and the emotional pain of knowing that I had to start from scratch. I had no foundation, no basis, and I had no meaning.

This is the infamous Christmas Day photo I took just outside her house on the 25th. I have used it in my stage presentations for the last two years.

Besides – the money in the bank had no meaning either (It was the first time in my life I had a six figure bank account!). The large flat had no meaning. The 50" plasma TV definitely had no meaning. What really was missing was a real relationship with someone that I could build on, someone I could trust. Like a child, that morning, I wept once more. And like a child, that morning, I threw away everything that was reminding me of our relationship. I destroyed the pictures that we made together. I threw away everything that had anything to do with her, but it didn't help how I felt, it didn't take away the pain.

At that moment in time, when I felt the loneliest since I was a young boy, I made a decision. Let me re-phrase that. I didn't make a decision. A decision was made for me. Something inside of me, as clear as a bell, spoke to me. I don't want you to freak out on me; I don't mean voices coming out of me and talking to me, but what I mean is that I had clarity. And this clarity can only happen in deep moments of inspiration or desperation. For me, it was the latter one.

I knew I would not compromise myself in the future in relationships. I knew I wouldn't compromise my 'soul' again. I would not compromise my ideals, what I stand for and what I stand against, and that gave me incredible strength and determination. It was Christmas Day, and I was alone. It was Christmas Day in 2008 when my life changed once more. Although I was perceived to be successful, from the outside, I knew that what really mattered was to be successful on the inside. That day was a turnaround for me to start living as who I really was. I finally understood that the true meaning of life is honesty to yourself and the people around you, the meaningful relationships you can create, and I was on my way to get myself just that.

Chapter 20

Dropping The Parachute

'Looking to blame some outside influence is counter-productive. It's you. Always has been. Always will be. Your efforts, your actions and your decisions are the only thing you should be concerned with. Don't seek other reasons, they don't exist.' Robert Cornish

After possibly the most confusing year of my entire life, I started 2009 with a new list of things to achieve. I accepted full responsibility for my situation and I wondered what to wish for. It was not that my wishes didn't come true, they actually became true in a frighteningly accurate manner. What I needed to work out was what was actually worth wishing for? So I wrote a list of the following things (people) I wanted for 2009:

1. a girlfriend that would understand me that I could love and look after (someone not complicated – as I was complicated enough for two)

2. a business partner who would take care of growing what I had built so far. I wasn't quite sure what I had, but I made money and that was surely a good thing.

3. a real business that I could leave alone and walk away from and possible run from somewhere sunny (no, not Spain!)

2009 started well. My speaking gig at the Wealth Intelligence Academy (previously know as Whitney, now Tigrent) at the end of January got me off on the right footing. I was looking forward to be sharing a stage with James Caan and Kevin Green (don't worry if you don't know who they are – I just wanted to drop some names of millionaires in here). Dan Bradbury's suggestions were put into place, as I created my first membership site, raised my prices and put some upsells in place.

Proof that rubbing shoulders with Billionaires works. Me and James Caan.

The gig at the end of January went really well, I had a laugh on stage and sold well, I met Martin Roberts from the BBC, who is now a business partner of mine in a joint venture with Ranjan (which will be a product on Auction Secrets released in Summer 2011). And to top it all one of Tina's friends I had spent some time with over Christmas, Gudrun, flew in to be my date for the weekend and that included a black tie charity event. She looked gorgeous and dazzling and made me look great.

Chapter 20

On stage at WIA, my biggest speaking gig so far. I loved it and the crowd loved me. Unbeknownst to me a lady by the name of Tamar Peters was amongst them, who booked me later that year on my biggest stage yet.

Oh, and the thing I almost thought would never happen: I quit my job in the middle of a recession. Gave back the company car, said good bye to share options and pension plan. I was finally dropping my parachute.

Looking back it was one of the best things I have ever done. And here is why. While I was in a job, I got my monthly paycheque which made me lazy (I know when you read this book I don't come across as a lazy guy). While I was in a job, I had to dance to someone else's tune, even if I didn't like it. While I was in a job, I had to pretend and scheme to build my own business alongside. In short, I wasn't free and I wasn't taking responsibility.

Towards the end of my time with HP I was 'cruising', to say the least. In the last few months of 2008 I had even hired a freelancer to do my work from my home office, while I was concentrating on my business!

Here is why I believe everyone should start their own business: It will be a free 24/7/365 course in self development, the end of blame, complain and justify because the bucks stops with you! Period.

Please make sure you don't just leave your job unless you have alternative income. At the stage I left my job, I had consistently made multiple times my income over more than a year.

Chapter 21

How I Started To Be-Lieve Again

'A man has only one escape from his old self: to see a different self in the mirror of some woman's eyes.' Clare Boothe Luce

January was a busy month, I lived now in my big empty penthouse apartment, with a massive plasma screen and the black leather sofas, and at least my seventeen year old son enjoyed it. His mates thought he was a right pimp. The weekend before the big speaking gig I had run another of my standard two day workshops in London. These workshops evolved from that original one day for £297 all the way to this two day £1,297 workshop, which included some of the product creation modules from the 'Digital Product Creation Bootcamp'.

Whenever I ran my weekend workshops in London, I decided to stay at the hotel we were running the workshops in, this time it was the Radisson Edwardian in Tottenham Court Road. There was a girl in the workshop I had a connection with, a little something, and I wanted to ask her to go to a club with me that evening. Somehow it just didn't happen, I was maybe a bit too forward and she bailed on me. I hadn't been out since I was a teenager I think, I definitely never had been to London for any other reason but to work or meditation. I was all ready to go out and enjoy myself, and not having a date would not stop me. The prospect of spending the

143

evening in the hotel with the delegates talking internet marketing, helped me as well to get myself a timeout magazine and look what I could be doing that night.

My eyes fell on a club I liked the sound of, and I went out and bought some suitable clothes, had some dinner and then arrived at the club around 10pm or so. It was weird. I felt totally out of place, like a vegetarian in a burger joint. I must have looked awkward and lost, because I attracted some sorry looks stumbling round the club. I remembered why I hated going out. I didn't know anyone, I didn't like the loud music or the choice of music and as people got more drunk and off their faces as the night progressed, I felt even less like them. I didn't drink much alcohol either, it didn't agree with me and since my liver infection I got drunk from just a scoop of rum and raisins ice cream.

I was about to leave, just doing one last round looking at faces and trying to work out what life was all about (a club on Saturday night is maybe not the place to do that), when two ladies noticed me and how lost I was. They introduced themselves as the owners of the club and showed me round. That was a different view all together, as they introduced me to some of their friends and I said a few hellos. My perception of the club suddenly changed, it looked a lot friendlier and with a drink in my hand, we headed for the dance floor. I loved dancing, just hadn't had much practice recently, but I got into the swing of it rather quickly.

I turned around and noticed two things: one, the ladies had left me on the dance floor by myself, and two, I saw a girl dancing by herself and dancing her heart out. It was almost as if a light emanated from her, a warm glow and sweet innocence exuded her, so different from anybody else. I was magnetically drawn to her and as magnets do, we attached ourselves to each other that night.

Chapter 21

Her name was Lieve and that was the first night of our beautiful relationship. I took her to my hotel that night and as much as I enjoyed it, I didn't think this one night adventure could turn into anything serious. But we hit it off big time, and we have been together now for over two years. Many times we have marvelled at the unlikely event that brought us together. A girlfriend that would understand me that I could love and look after? Tick.

Lieve and I getting ready to go out to a club in February 2009

Life surely is a mysterious thing, but here is one clue I got from my limited experience: if you want something, you got to ask for it. Jim Rohn used to say: 'the miracle is set up. You knock and it will be opened, you sow and you shall reap, you ask and it will be given.'

Being with Lieve is just like I always imagined a relationship should be. No hard work, just flow, openness and acceptance and sweet, sweet caring love for each other. She brings out the best in me, period. I finally have balance in my life, as we take time out for each other and enjoy doing things together, something I never allowed myself to do before. Now I know it's the journey that's the most precious and there is no arriving.

But let me quote Jim once more: 'You look after yourself for me and I look after myself for you'.

Lieve and I in Cyprus in Spring 2010. Happy Days.

And I am glad I kept searching, because it would have been a mighty shame to settle for anything less.

Chapter 22

Getting Serious

'It is difficult, but not impossible, to conduct strictly honest business.'
Mahatma Gandhi

Because of my success on stage at the end of January I had two workshops totally sold out. I had sold a three day version of the course and I prepared my 'upsell'. I was aware that after a three day intensive, most people will have seen the potential but also realised how much more there is to 'building the machine'. My idea was a one year continuation programme with monthly meetings and a membership site and support through experts. I offered this at £497 a month, or at a generous 40% discount of £2,970 a year. I had an amazing uptake and had my recurring income through a hight ticket coaching programme in place.

In March I also had a some new joiners to my Platinum programme, a lovely couple by the name of Watson. James and his wife Licia. James was a fellow member in Dan Bradbury's group, but wanted to learn more about the internet side of things. He stood out from all the students through his eager participation and willingness to help and learn, and within two months I promoted him to be an 'expert' on the team. Experts were in essence friends and ex-students, who gave up their time and expertise for free to help other platinum students in exchange of being part of the group and hanging out with me.

James and I started to talk every day and I noticed that he had qualities I was missing. He had great complimentary skills and it was only in September 2010 when Mike Southon pointed out that James was my 'foil', something that was reconfirmed when we did the Wealth Dynamics test in January 2011, when we were totally on opposite sides of the square. James an accumulator, me a star 'Creator'.

I ran 'MyInternetMarketingTutor.com' happily but was intrigued by the prospect of starting an additional business with James and leveraging his skills. I loved working with someone, and we spend many long days in Bath at his home planning and sketching out the new business. The brand was just half a year old and it was designed to grow and remove me from the logo, as all previous logos were my face and different names.

This brand was supposed to last me for years.

By July we had formed 'YourInternetBuddies.com', and we designed a multi-tier membership site with Platinum and four more levels, which we finally launched in September 2009.

Chapter 22

This logo and brand for 'Your Internet Buddies – let's make money online – together...' replaced 'My Internet Marketing Tutor' in Autumn 2009. It was designed via a contest on 99designs.com and was an antidote to all the 'academy', 'school' and 'university' brands. I'm on the left, James is on the right.

The main reason behind a worldwide, dollar-based, low-cost , online coaching offering was that I felt that my workshops were clearly geographically limited. The Platinum level, although enjoyable and profitable, was only offered to workshop graduates, which was a very small number of people and not really scalable.

The success underlying the Gold Coaching launch was 'The Most Insane $1,702 FREE Gift Ever' combined with a $1 dollar trial to our $97 Gold Coaching Programme. It was my first product launch and 're-cycled' some of my existing products like the 'Instant Internet Cash System', 'Secret Shortcuts', 'Digital Product Creation Secrets', 'Grilling The Experts' and my 'Killer Squeeze Page Generator' Software as a gift and ethical bribe.

Once we had tested and improved the conversion process, we launched it on a wider scale to some of our joint venture partners in November. We generated $10,000 a month in recurring income in the first few weeks of the launch, which equated to just a bit more than 100 members. James, who was working full time as a sales man for a software company at this stage, took the audacious plunge into self employment after just six months of working with me at the end of 2009.

The opt-in page of the YourInternetBuddies.com Gold Coaching Programme September 2009. We still use a very similar optin page today.

Chapter 22

I loved working with a business partner and I felt that by doing what I do best and being able to bounce ideas and split tasks I could achieve more than ever.

James is an avid student of 'the other Dan' (Dan Kennedy) and we started to experiment with offline marketing and a monthly newsletter to our members. My graphic design and printing background came in handy.

And I remembered my wish list from the beginning of the year. A business partner who would take care of growing what I had built so far? Tick.

Chapter 23

Becoming What You Are

'I don't care what you think, I don't care what you say, I only care about what you do – that will tell me everything about you.'
Dennis Cummins

I had worked hard in the first half of the year, but I felt a strange loss of energy and lustre when I was planning my future. It was to be Harv Eker again (again not him in person but through one of his courses) that I found another missing stone from the mosaic that was to become the complete me. I felt a hundred times better than the previous years, more and more confident that I was enough, that my intrinsic and god given 'talent' was fuelling my journey to some predefined fulfilling destination.

I had heard a lot about the 'Enlightened Warrior Camp' and to be honest, when I heard the name I thought it sounded a bit weird. I even thought that it made no sense, a contradiction in its name and a dichotomy of beliefs. A hardened pacifist and hippy, I could not really relate to the word 'warrior' at all. Peaks (this is what delegates and attendees of Peak Potentials workshops call the company lovingly) have sent an info pack through the post and I openly admit that I didn't read it.

I had signed up for the course after my 'train the trainer' experience in October 2007 and I had bailed out from doing it in 2008. I was with Patrizia in Croatia at the naturist beach, so becoming an 'Enlightened Warrior' was not on my to-do list. And to be frank, it wasn't on my list for 2009 either, but they told me that I would not be able to delay it again. And as I had paid $4,000 or so for the course, I thought I might as well. I tell you this because it is amazing how we 'think' we make decisions and how we really end up doing things!

So I flew to the US in summer 2009, into the unknown, slightly unsure of what to expect. I can tell you for free that I don't like people telling me what to do, I still had a bit of a hangover from my religious group experience and I got a bit cynical about the self development world. The main reason was that since my first experience with Tony Robbins in 2005 I had met so many people that attend all the events they can get to and they can (and many times can't) afford – but they still don't seem to get anywhere. I don't want to sound harsh, but this is how I felt about the industry. I also had some 'behind the scenes' knowledge now, being one of the speakers from stage and it made me a bit disillusioned.

I arrived at the airport in New York and found the shuttle that I had booked from here in the UK. We picked up about ten people from the different airports, all of them with 'destination warrior camp'. I didn't like it. I wanted to go home! I wanted my comfort zone. Little did I know that this was the beginning of a week I would never forget.

We arrived in a massive hotel complex in a remote nature park and at registration were assigned to our rooms, including our new 'buddies' for the week. The atmosphere was unsettled and you could feel people's restlessness and nervousness. I think there were about two hundred and fifty of us, from all over the US and the rest of the world. About seventy percent women I guess, or maybe I just focused more on them.

Chapter 23

This evening in the great hall, our trainer, Dennis Cummins, addressed us and told us what was to come. I was speechless, it was the same Dennis that I saw in 2006 when I did my first Millionaire Mind Intensive. He did a short slot as a Co-Trainer, and I remember thinking that he was a bit of a wally and I frankly thought he was useless! The man on stage today was impressive. I almost didn't recognise him. Poise, power, leadership and charisma. Whatever he is taking, I wanted some of it.

It was clear within the first few hours that they'll work us hard. I would really, really love to give you a detailed account of every day of the camp, but as part of the camp you swear that you won't, so I can't. I can though, describe one small experience of what happened to me in the course of thirty minutes one evening later that week.

First though, listen to this bit of self talk: 'I am lazy, I am week, I am average. I am selfish and I have a big ego. I am a coward and avoid confrontation.' That is how I started out and that is how I saw myself for most of my life. This was my mindset and it got me to where I was in August 2009.

We were given a little diary that I have in front of me now. I am reading through some of my entries and the experiences and notes indicate breakthroughs that have been transformational. Over the next four days I have worked more on myself and harder than in my whole life, I pushed myself to limits I didn't dream possible of ever achieving, physically and mentally. I felt deep and profound love for strangers, I connected to the core of all human beings, I found the warrior inside of me that would fight against and sacrifice for injustice. I discovered compassionate leadership in myself and I was forced to step up to the plate. I learned how to handle fear and doubt. I walked on fire, I sang and danced and laughed and cried, I sharpened my mind and understanding of life and human beings and I became an 'Enlightened Warrior', connected to my inner power. And I felt alive and drunken on life! Aho!

My diary from the EWC in Summer 2009, documenting one of the best weeks of my life. Who says self development courses don't work?

Everyday was an incredible adventure, but I want to share a breakthrough on the third evening, when we played a game called 'the beauty I see in you is...'. At this stage we had overcome and endured all kinds of hardship, challenges and adventure together.

Chapter 23

The group was split into two and we sat on two rows of opposing chairs. So I was sitting opposite, very closely, one of my fellow warriors and looked him in the eyes. My sentence had to start with 'the beauty I see in you is...' and I had to tell what beauty I saw in him in thirty second.

I can tell you that my mind freaked out telling a bloke what 'beauty I saw in him'! He then had to say the same to me. Then he would move one chair to the left and I sat opposite the next person, who again said to me 'the beauty I see in you is...'

Before I tell you the outcome I want you to get how unusual it is to tell a stranger what beauty you see in them. Our brains and minds are incredibly perceptive and you can detect truth and genuine emotion. And when you put yourself on the spot, something from deep inside will come up with an answer. Not your thinking brain, something different. You can't prepare, you have to start to read people, because if you make stuff up or bullshit them they'd know. How do I know? Because I knew when they just wanted to get it over with and made something up.

So what amazed me was not just that I was finding it easier and easier to see the beauty and truth in the person opposite me, but I was blown away what literally everyone saw in me (apart from the few that were making stuff up). By the end my tears were flowing freely as the doors to my heart were flung wide open.

'The beauty I see in you is courage, leadership, strength and compassion'. Wow! By the 20th person I thought 'bloody hell, if they ALL see it, maybe I am missing something. Maybe I don't see myself the way the rest of the world does!' What a revelation.

What I love about Peaks is that their products are great. Their stuff works. It's not for everyone, and it's not cheap. This is what I took away for me and my business. I want my stuff to work. I don't want it to be for everyone and I don't want it to be cheap. Peaks are a hard selling company. Day five I was in peak state, fulfilled and happy and with an amazing sense of achievement and proof that their stuff works. So what better moment to sell me their $14,000 'Quantum Leap Programme'? I have seen the pitches, I have done the close myself, but I still ran to the back and signed up. And why not?

The Experience of the 'Enlightened Warrior Camp' has changed my life forever. When I came back to the UK I vowed to embrace leadership and would start to accept that I can lead a 'tribe', that people look to me for compassionate guidance. I started to watch my own videos to learn to see what they see. I create products that 'work', I don't want to please everyone, but look for my people. I know my value.

And above all, I became who I already was all along.

Chapter 24

Deserve And Need

'Life doesn't respond to need, it responds to deserve.' Jim Rohn

A simple concept and a phrase I repeated many times. Yet in my heart of hearts I didn't feel I 'deserved' success and wealth and all that. When the phone rang I still thought 'oh oh. what's wrong now?' instead of 'awesome, that'll be great news!' Money and success doesn't come to people who need it the most, it comes to those who 'deserve it'. This might not seem fair, but that's the way it is. This is not based on a moral or ethical deservedness, but more on an understanding of market, money, and the laws governing them.

It was the end of my year with Dan Bradbury and one of the promises I had made to myself when joining Dan's group was that I would not just 'make my money back', but I also was determined to win the 'Better Your Best' competition. The coach or trainer that can demonstrate the most progress made within the twelve months of the programme, can win a year in an Aston Martin.

I really have to thank Dan for giving me the chance to present. I wasn't gonna do it at first, because I didn't want to be used as a sales pitch for Dan's programme. Not that his programme wasn't good, I just felt that it was only for a specific kind of person and I saw that many people did not succeed. Dan encouraged me to come for 'me', not for 'him'. I couldn't believe what a year I had. It was only because of Dan that I actually sat down and worked out what I had done each month. I was impressed myself. I was so obsessed with what was still missing that I almost didn't see what I had achieved.

I was nominated as one of the three finalists and had twenty minutes to convince an audience to vote for me. I was very unsure of my chances, but I knew that I had to make an emotional appeal and not try to impress them with numbers. I went on last and I knew that I had be good, because one of the other finalists, Tom Breeze, was not just a handsome devil, he was also a public speaking coach, who had a great year as well.

One of the challenges I had encountered in my public speaking career that I had a little problem with time keeping at times, as I love to be spontaneous and 'free flowing' in my presentations. This time I had exactly twenty minutes and I had to rehearse to get it right. The trial run the night before didn't go well. Forty five minutes.

I also realised that I was throwing around some big numbers. £20K here, £15K there and so on... I then had this (dare I say myself) great idea to introduce a currency they all could relate to: a Pizza Day. 1PD (one pizza day) was worth £50, and that was what I got paid back then in Slough driving round delivering Pizzas.

I also used a lot of humour and interaction with the audience. One of my key lines was 'do I deserve?' and everyone whole heartedly agreed that I did deserve whatever I desired. The last slide was a picture of me outside the Aston showroom, asking if I deserved it.

Chapter 24

I did win the Aston with over 80% of all votes. If you are interested in how I structured the presentation, go to http://myjourneyandthemachine.com. There are some useful marketing and persuasion tips in there.

Dan handing me the keys of the Aston. Although this was total proof that I deserved an Aston, I still felt embarrassed, took the money instead and drove off in my VW Tiguan. If I won today, I'd take the Aston!

The same month I was invited to speak at the Ultimate Marketing Seminar, where I addressed an audience of almost a thousand people. Tamar Peters, who heard and saw me at WIA in January, had arranged for me to be one of the speakers along an illustrious line up of world class speakers and marketers. Some of the same names I had interviewed in the back room just two years earlier.

I became tearful on stage more than once as I told my story, from overcoming disappointments and failures to the people who had believed in me at a time when I didn't. I cried when I showed a photo of my dad, and I got so carried away that I overran massively. I offered my craziest offer yet, the 'Three Years In Three Days' workshop, where I attempted to teach everything I had learned in the last three years, from my first workshop in September 2006 all the way to that day.

On stage with a picture of my children Siddhartha and Aparna (she has recently changed her name to Alice), who were both in the audience supporting me. Another tearful moment.

I sold well, and I was surrounded by people who had 'connected' with me based on my story, not how much I had earned with my internet marketing. I know I upset some of the other 'hard nosed' speakers, but I was happy with what I had achieved.

A week later I presented in Dublin and I was the best selling speaker there. The Irish weren't too keen on the Americans or the English I guess and they don't like the hype. So I was a good fit.

Chapter 24

I filled two workshops from the two speaking events and James and I decided that we would stop running workshops with the end of 2009. The new offer was a ninety day coaching programme with Platinum at its core, in my eyes a much better chance for people to succeed.

Chapter 25

Where In The World?

'All that we are is the result of what we have thought. The mind is everything. What we think we become.' Gautama Buddha

My divorce had come through earlier this summer and I started to look at the possibility of living abroad. I had consistently worked on the vision of my business, the 'machine', that would serve me and feed me wherever I was, so why not be somewhere else? I was also thinking of speaking less from the stage. Not that I didn't like it – I loved it – but there was something that bothered me about the seminar and public selling industry and I wasn't sure I wanted to be part of it.

So with the limitations of having to be back in the UK at least once a month for Platinum and my kids, where could I go? So looking for sunshine and a bit of Englishness, I could only think of Malta. I convinced James and Licia (it didn't take much convincing to leave the UK in October) to join me and Lieve for a 'working' holiday with the prospect of moving to Malta.

We liked it a lot, we rented a big villa with pool and worked on our wireless laptops as if we were at home, just better. One of my talks, 'Fear Flip Fundamentals – How To Use Your Fear To Achieve Your Dreams' was conceived and recorded in Malta by the pool. Largely based on my last few years of experiences and Harv's strategies I learned at the Enlightened Warrior camp.

You can download the presentation from the book's website for free. Just go to http://myjourneyandthemachine.com

Malta was sunny and had some englishness, but as much as I liked it as a holiday, I didn't want to live there. Sometimes you just get a feeling.

I had attended another one of Mark Anastasi's events in the UK some weeks before we went to Malta and heard Mark Vurnum speak. Mark V (as we call him to separate him form Mark A) sounded convincing and I liked what he offered, so I invited him to speak to my Platinum group. I had arranged an extended training session and invited anyone from my list who was interested to come and join us. We sold out the event in no time and Mark V sold his £2,000 product well. I made some good commissions and I took Mark V up on his offer to have a consultation with him in his home in Cyprus. Mark appeared very successful and his software looked like the missing piece for unlimited traffic we were looking for. If his story added up, then he was making eight figures a year. Definitely a guy I would want to learn from. So best to hang out, spend some time and take things further after that.

James and I flew out to Cyprus in November and I made sure I had booked an appointment with Mark A as well, making the most of my time out there in Pafos. I also thought it might potentially be a place to live.

The session with Mark V was disappointing and brought up some issues for James and I. We didn't see any real numbers, no bank accounts, no multimillion dollar business and surely no golden nuggets strategy. It was a reminder that I was still distracted by shiny objects from actually building a real business.

Chapter 25

The experience was relevant for multiple reasons though: Firstly, never promote something or someone unless you have used and tested their product and seen the results. Secondly, there is NO missing piece or ultimate tool or answer to fix your problems. Thirdly, things are always harder than you think and take longer than you would expect.

The meeting with Mark A was great though. We did a short video for his list to promote the Gold Coaching programme and I warmed to the thought of living in Cyprus. It was middle of November and I got a sunburn from driving in the cabriolet I had rented.

Mark Anastasi and I in Limassol pondering universal questions on life, death and conspiracy. The video was part of very successful launch sequence to his list, with one of the highest earnings per click Mark has ever experienced. This laid the foundation for his incredible support for our Blueprint Coaching Programme launch in July 2010.

Before we flew back , we had a great dinner with the two Marks and partners and Roy Carter and Lyn, who was an estate agent specialising in villas in Cyprus.

Christmas 2009? Don't worry – it was all good. I spent it with Lieve, James and Licia before we flew off to Austria. Because I had shared my story from stage a few times, I even had a list of people who offered me to spend Christmas with them, most of them I had never met! What an amazing world we are living in.

I liked Cyprus and when I returned I told Lieve all about it. We booked a flight in January and explored the possibility of living there. Lyn showed us three places and we decided on a great two bedroom flat overlooking the sea with pool in a very quite area.

We moved out on 1st March and loved it, loved it, loved it. I flew back once a month for Platinum, my kids and speaking gigs. Living there was great. Working from there was easy as well. I never actually really believed it to be possible, whatever you hear. But when I experienced it for myself, you do wonder why you would spend your time in a cold and rainy place. Or as I jokingly say 'If you can work from anywhere in the world, why work from your home in England?'

James and I organised the 'Traffic and Conversion Summit', a sold out one day event dedicated to traffic and conversion (you might have guessed it) with an ulterior motive in mind. The six sessions from the day were to become the high value bonuses for our first big launch in July. We used direct mail for the first time sending our postcards and also produced a free report as a viral tool.

I flew in from Cyprus with Lieve and as we drove to the event early that Saturday, I was rammed by a truck on the motorway. Our little rental car was destroyed and it's a miracle we escaped without injury. I arrived, with the tow truck, just in time to change into my suit and with the opening words: "Good morning. I am glad to be here!"

Learnings from the accident. Many things in your life you don't control. You never know when your time has come, so live with passion and integrity. And I will not buy or rent a small car again.

A week later I was invited to speak at Rob Moore's Property Super Conference along James Caan again and many other great speakers. I sold a six week webinar course on Lead Generation, which I ran from Cyprus in my swimming trunks (sounds better than underpants). I loved it.

Tim Ferris referred to this as the millionaire lifestyle. Mobility and time freedom. Things were looking up.

Chapter 26

The $250,000 Month

'Luck is what happens when preparation meets opportunity.' Seneca

We were working on a new coaching programme that was to include all that we had learned over the last four years and make it available to anyone at a low price worldwide. For months we worked tirelessly on the concepts and content and in July 2010 we launched the BlueprintCoachingProgram.com.

We had a great model in Lee McIntyre's membership site and we took time to prepare. As I mentioned earlier, we put an event on in April just to create special high value bonuses. I created a unique report sharing the 'Clickbank Quick Cash Strategy', which was a free way to make money and I lined up all possible JV partners to support me. James and I also copied Frank Kern's idea to offer a two day event a few months down the line as a bonus for people signing up. We called it the 'Six Figure Formula'.

We achieved something called 'momentum', which is self perpetuating. There is also a little know principle in branding that states: 'Visibility = Credibility', which simply means if people see your stuff all the time they assume it's great! Both these factors helped us greatly in achieving this result.

It was our first proper launch in those two weeks of July 2010, and we had a lot of other firsts as well. It was the first time we had a webinar lockout with 1,142 on the webinar (over 3,500 had registered). We had a great converting offer and turned over more than $170,000 for the first time with our first official worldwide product. It put us on the map! Was it easy? Nope, not at all. Did we learn something? You bet. We did a lot of things right, and I guess that success is just doing more right than wrong.

James, Lee McIntyre and I at his workshop in Newcastle of all places. I guess Lee wanted to make sure he only had committed people there.

The launch was so successful that our planned 'Six Figure Formula' event, where we wanted to teach people how we built and launched our multi six figure business, had be re-named to the '7-Figure-Formula', as we were now on track to be a million dollar a year business. It was a buzz and it is shocking how quickly you adjust to new levels of income or success. Within a few weeks it became just normal. This is what stretching your comfort zone is all about. The massive stumbling block of a few months ago is the small hurdle of today.

As crazy as it sounds, I had a second launch in the same month going on, as Rob Moore and I offered the 'Lead Generator

Chapter 26

Masterclass' home study course to his list via a webinar launch. I prepared it all from Cyprus and we did over $50,000 worth of sales from just one webinar with follow up. With some other income from affiliate sales and our other product sales, it was our first $250,000 month.

I had decided to come back from Cyprus for the summer, as it was getting far too hot there and somehow I felt that I might not return.

August was dealing with hundreds of new clients and learning that every transaction has a maintenance trail. You don't just sell a quarter million dollars of product, you also got to fulfil this stuff! We worked pretty much flat out and prepared for our the final part of the launch – the '7-Figure-Formula'.

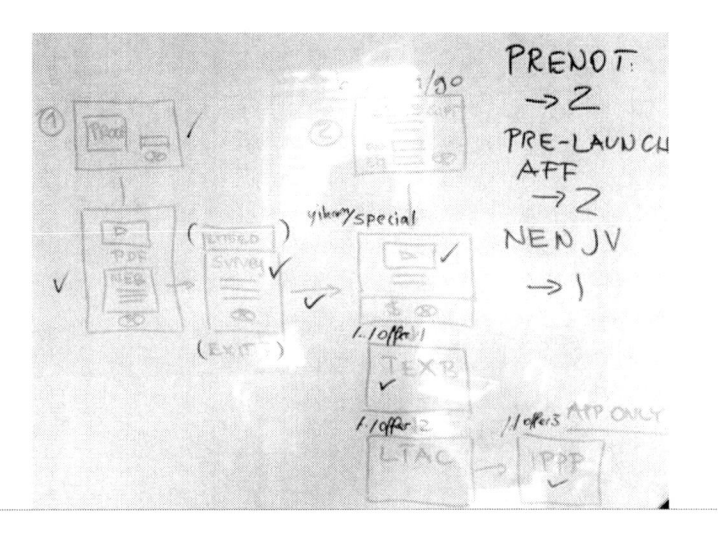

The 'Blueprint Coaching Programme' launch layout on the white board. The prospect's journey starts on the left top corner and ends in an application process for the 'Instant Profit Partner Programme'.

173

Chapter 27

The £100,000 Weekend

'If I had eight hours to chop down a tree, I'd spend six hours sharpening my ax'. Abraham Lincoln

I believe that you create your own luck. I also believe that you find and express what is unique about you and your business. So when James and I planned the '7-Figure-Formula' event, we did model from some people, but we also made sure it was distinctly our own. We made sure it had my character and what I stand for in every aspect of it.

The idea is simple. A special two day event only for our best clients, a 'customer appreciation event' at the end of their completed coaching programme. I would invite my millionaire friends to speak, pay for a celebrity guest speaker as well and make everyone feel good about themselves.

We would stage a competition and let the audience reward our most successful student (a la Dan Bradbury's 'Better Your Best' competition) and offer a high ticket (£10,000 a year) coaching programme on application only basis.

Add more bonuses over the two days and drop the price towards the end and you have your result. In our case, our £100,000 weekend. There are a lot of moving parts to this equation, but if you have a list of buyers and fans, you can achieve this amazing feat quite easily.

The event cost around £20,000, with the prize for the competition winner and all the marketing and freebies included. This time though, unlike at the launch of Blueprint Coaching, there were no affiliates to pay. This was cash in the bank. The event was a massive success for us and from the feedback of the 250 clients in the room they felt the same.

My first eight page direct mail sales letter that I wrote for the event. Download the full letter at http://myjourneyandthemachine.com

You know the guest speakers by now. They are all intrinsically involved in my story and success. Rob Moore, Dan Bradbury, Ranjan Bhattacharya and Mike Southon added tremendous value to my and James' presentations. All of us had just with one single aim: to make everyone in the audience realise that they could have whatever they wanted if they were ready to go after it.

Chapter 27

Our own objective was to launch a new 'super level' coaching and mentoring programme called the 'Inner Circle Mastermind Programme'. We were looking for ten people but ended up accepting sixteen from over forty applications that we split into two groups.

We only accepted people with businesses that we knew we could help increase turnover and profit. Our aim was to have a 100% success rate from our personal coaching students.

Me on stage at the '7 Figure Formula' with Better Your Best competition winner Maksud Rahman (centre with cheque) and finalists Keith Watson, Phill Turner and Gillian Fox. All other finalists joined the 'Inner Circle Mastermind Programme' that weekend.

Chapter 28

Expanding Horizons

'Our business in life is not to get ahead of others, but to get ahead of ourselves – to break our own records, to outstrip our yesterday by our today.' Stewart B. Johnson

When I was in the corporate world I sometimes heard about people being 'head hunted'. I never was. So I was very flattered when I was approached in October 2010 by Stuart Ross, a guy I admired for his achievements and straight talking. I heard him present at Chris Cobb's event in June 2010 and I as quite impressed. I understood that he was successful in marketing high ticket coaching programmes and systems, and that he had built a membership site with over thousand members. I noticed he was running something called the 'Six Figure Mentors' and I liked the look of it. This young (under thirty is young for me), Porsche driving go-getter with high aspirations invited me for lunch in Windsor to talk.

I was blown away when he offered me the opportunity to become an equal partner in TheSixFigureMentors.com. My only reservation was my existing relationship with James and my existing commitments to my clients, but the rest of it sounded great.

When I joined Stuart officially in November 2010 we started preparing for the imminent launch of the membership site that promised to become a 'One Stop Marketing System'. Our plan is to grow the business to 3,000 members by the end of 2011 and I am confident that some of the unique benefits and features in our offer will help us achieve that.

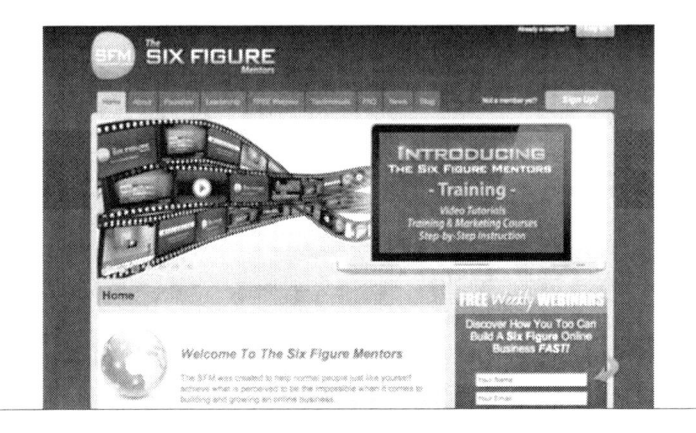

The official SFM website February 2011. Built for scale, we got big plans for 2011.

The pre-launch in the beginning of December was very successful and we started our first month with 250 members. I have moved back to a bigger house in Bracknell and we are renting offices with staff and our first operations manager. Over the years I have learned a few things about running a sustainable business and building a 'machine', and I want to make sure that every part of the Six Figure Mentors is scalable and ultimately can work without me being there. It also serves my larger purpose, sharing the knowledge of internet marketing, which has saved and changed my life so drastically, with the widest possible audience.

Chapter 28

We got great plans for the Six Figure Mentors and I have been lucky to be able to dedicate and invest my time for the last four months building some great foundations. All I can say is: watch this space.

Chapter 29

Words And Deeds

'Since you get more joy out of giving joy to others, you should put a good deal of thought into the happiness that you are able to give.' Eleanor Roosevelt

Just before Christmas I flew to Austria to surprise my dad who celebrated his eightieth birthday. It's great when you have freedom to just jump on the plane and leave, not having to ask anyone. He was really moved. My dad had a bit of a hard time in the last few years. He had three strokes, one of them affecting his speech centre in the brain, which for him, a former radio presenter, was hard.

My dad is a very private person, old school, never shows his feelings, so I am not sure where my genes of public exhibitionism come from. I was never close to him, he wasn't the dad who was around much. He worked a lot and didn't spend much time with his kids. I never missed it until I reflected on it as a grown up. As a kid I thought my parents were perfect, as most of us do. It's just the way it is.

When I visited him in hospital last year, after his third stroke, it was just him and me in the room. He looked frail, he had lost a lot of weight. I sat with him, and I wanted to talk, really talk, no small talk. About him and me, how I loved him and how I knew he did the best he could. There was no way to introduce that kind of topic, so I just told him. It was the first time he told me he loved me too and that he was proud of me. Oh boy, two grown men crying in harmony, what an image. I couldn't believe how much I had craved that approval from my dad. It's something so deep, so fundamental for all of us to have this approval, and many of us never get it. I am glad I had this conversation with him before it was too late.

Me and dad in Austria in 2008. My relationship with him is not as close as I would like it to be, but I have come to accept it.

At the end of January 2011, we had a two day retreat for our 'Inner Circle Mastermind Group' the dedicated group that had invested £5,000 for a six month mentoring and coaching programme with me and James.

It was at the four month mark of the six months programme, and we asked everyone to prepare a progress report that they would present to the group. It was for the first time both groups were together and I had invited John Williams and Tom Breeze as guest speakers. John talked on Wealth Dynamics, and everyone did the

Chapter 29

profiling test that helped them to see their strengths and their easiest way to wealth. Tom did a presentation on using video for marketing, another very useful session.

For me though, the most rewarding and enlightening part of the weekend were people's progress reports. As you know from my story, I have tried many ways to pass on the knowledge of marketing using the internet that has not only changed my life, but saved my life from mediocrity. Listening to success story after success story, I realised I had finally succeeded.

Here were people, who had made £3,000 a month when they started working with my who now turn over £15,000, there is a business owner who from making £250,000 is expecting to make £1,000,000, and there are also some who just started and made their first money. But all of them were proof and testimony of what I stood for and believed in. That you can change your life through Internet Marketing.

James and I thought it would be the perfect moment to ask if people would like to continue with the coaching programme after March and we had an incredible 80% signup rate.

Seeing people succeed and break free from their jobs, being part of their journey and witnessing their progress has been the most satisfying experience in all my years of aiming to bring the knowledge of marketing and internet marketing to the world. Every one of them shared their story and the one common theme was that their business success was linked with their personal journey of self discovery and self development.

I have uploaded some of the videos from the event to the website, they are awesome and you can check them out if you want, at http://myjourneyandthemachine.com

I also invited a professional photographer, Dianna Bonner to take portraits of everyone, and the weekend was an amazing experience for everyone.

I tried to work out the best way to do this, so here are the 'Inner Circle Mastermind Members of 2011' starting from the left: Phill, Guy, John, Licia, Lieve, Alan, James, Daniel Chris, Robin, Gillian, Stuart, Keith, Rick, Eileen, Anthony, Satnam, Suzanne, Christian, Andrew, Lisa, Richard and Satie. Missing on this photo: Kathryn and Paul

Chapter 30

The End

'And in the end, the love you take is equal to the love you make.'
The Beatles

The question I ask myself all the time, something Tony Robbins calls your primary question, is: 'How can I help more people in a better way with less of my time?' I have learned that when you focus on helping people, solve their problems and provide them with answers, money will follow. (Providing you have built the 'machine'!)

With 'TheSixFigureMentors.com' on one end of the spectrum (a $97 a month coaching and training site) and the £10,000 a year Inner Circle Mastermind Programme on the other end, I can help the maximum amount of people get started but I am also able to spend some of my time on one-to-one coaching and in small group masterminding.

Ultimately, it can't be just about the money, this is why I urge you to put a system in place so that money is not a problem anymore. It took some time, but I look at the current businesses and income streams and I realise that I have built the 'machine'. I can coach a few people personally, but my income doesn't depend on it, I have thousands of members (safety in numbers) paying me every month, allowing for good cash flow predictions, but again, my business and income doesn't depend on it. Thirdly I have all these great projects and promotions with partners and friends keeping me excited, making up another part of my income, and you guessed it, my income and business doesn't depend on it either.

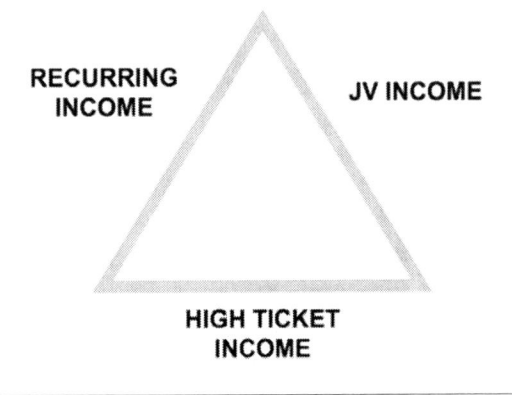

```
                    ▲
                   / \
   RECURRING      /   \     JV INCOME
   INCOME        /     \
                /       \
               /         \
              /_____\
              HIGH TICKET
                INCOME
```

This is what Stuart and I call the 'Ultimate Income Model', where a third of your money comes from 'Recurring Income', like a membership site, a third comes from 'Joint Venture' promotions and affiliate income, and one third comes from 'High Ticket' income like coaching or workshops.

Am I happy? Happiness is a fleeting muse and I can say that I enjoy her presence frequently. But the question I ask myself is about contentment. Am I content? With what I learned, with what I achieved, with my life? The answer is yes, because writing this book, I have found that I have given my best, wasn't afraid to fail or be a fool for love. I have learned to like the crazy Austrian that wants to make people laugh and cares so much about what people think about him. I am on a journey, this is a milestone. I have come this far, and I am not gonna stop until my last breath will leave my body and people will say 'he's given it all'! And as far as I am

Chapter 30

concerned, you got to give it all, because there is no holding back, no second chance, no rehearsals – this is it.

My next steps? I will keep speaking on stage and sharing my knowledge, I want to inspire people to not accept their status quo and make them believe that they can change and have whatever they want and be whoever they want to be.

Next week I will be on stage with Lord Alan Sugar (don't worry if you don't know who he is, just wanted to name drop). I will share my story and I will be looking for people who get what I am about – then we can do some business together.

There is no work life balance, there's only life.

Make your work what you love and you will never work again.

Let people know what you stand for, what you stand against.

I learned a lot about the 'machine'. About all the moving parts of it; all the parts that are generating money from many different income streams, flowing into my accounts while I sleep or while I'm awake. What started as a dream when I was a child – freedom, love, and choice – and what took me the best part of forty years of my life to achieve, has finally come into existence. And if you have read the story, you will know that it didn't come easy.

It won't stop here, because it never stops. We dedicate the most precious thing we have to our endeavours – our time. So I would urge you to do all you can to look deep inside yourself to make sure it's an endeavour you consider worthwhile. It's different for all of us, but we all need meaning and purpose to live a fulfilled life.

Let me fuse a few words of wisdom of my mentors into my own: "If the why is clear, and if the what is clear, the how will become easy because you will not stop, you will not falter, you will not give in and give up until you have achieved what you set out to do; but it is the journey and not the goal that creates the memories and stories that set our hearts on fire and inspire our minds".

One of my friends and Inner Circle students, Guy Fisher, is working on an amazing project that helps people find their life's purpose. I was lucky enough to be one of the first few to take the online version of Richard Jacobs' 'What's Your Purpose' test. So after all this time, all the trials, all the tests and tribulations, it boiled down to just eight words: I serve the purpose of: "Creating harmony and lead people to happier lives." – Nice!

I had a slow start; I had many obstacles, and let me guess, you might have your own share of trouble, too! Life is short – so here is my advice: Suck it up and get on with it. Do it now!

Resources

'Grab Your £397 Worth Of Free Bonuses Now!'

(strictly time limited offer)

As a special thank you there are many amazing free bonuses and resources for you on our website:

simply go to: http://MyJourneyAndTheMachine.com

Here is what you will get, totally free of charge:

- The complete audio book of
  'My Journey & The Machine' read by the author

- Songs written by Daniel Wagner
  (including 'Lonely' and 'Harvest')

- Detailed breakdown of
  'How I Won The Aston Martin' presentation

- The 6 Bonus Chapters 'The Machine' with
  all components and explained in detail

- 'Fear Flip Fundamentals – use your fear
  to achieve your dreams' audio

- The '21 Day Fast' videos

and lots more...

Do it now before it's too late!
Go to http://MyJourneyAndTheMachine.com